AF715912

Supply Chain Management and its Applications in Computer Science

FOCUS SERIES

Series Editor Jean-Charles Pomerol

Supply Chain Management and its Applications in Computer Science

Saoussen Krichen
Sihem Ben Jouida

iSTE

WILEY

First published 2016 in Great Britain and the United States by ISTE Ltd and John Wiley & Sons, Inc.

ISTE Ltd
27-37 St George's Road
London SW19 4EU
UK

www.iste.co.uk

John Wiley & Sons, Inc.
111 River Street
Hoboken, NJ 07030
USA

www.wiley.com

Library of Congress Control Number: 2015954429

British Library Cataloguing-in-Publication Data
A CIP record for this book is available from the British Library
ISSN 2051-2481 (Print)
ISSN 2051-249X (Online)
ISBN 978-1-84821-871-0

Contents

List of Figures

List of Tables

Glossary

CFP	coalition formation problem
CLP	continuous linear programming
CS	coalition structure
CSG	coalition structure generation
CVRP	capacitated vehicle routing problem
DM	decision maker
DSS	decision support system
EOQ	economic order quantity
HC	holding cost
HVRP	heterogeneous fleet vehicle routing problem
GA	genetic algorithm
ILP	integer linear programming
MIP	mixed integer programming
OC	ordering cost
PD	payoff division
PDP	pick-up and delivery problem
PC	purchasing cost
SC	supply chain
SCM	supply chain management
TC	total cost
TS	tabu search
VRP	vehicle routing problem
VRPTW	vehicle routing problem with time windows
WP	warehousing problem

Introduction

A supply chain (SC) is a network of different entities or nodes (suppliers, manufacturers, distribution centers, warehouses, stores, etc.) that provide materials, transform them into intermediate or finished products and deliver them to customers to satisfy market requests. Among others, two main factors characterize an SC node: the demand and the productive capacity. The definition of these parameters usually requires a huge effort in terms of data collection. In effect, the information management related to demand and productive capacity is a very complex task characterized by a great number of critical issues: market needs (volumes and production ranges), industrial processes (machine downtimes and transportation modes) and supplies (part quality and delivery schedules). The market demand and the productive capacity also generate a flow of items and finances toward and from the SC nodes. Needless to say, the SC management takes care of the above mentioned issues, studying and optimizing the flow of materials, information and finances along the entire SC. The main goal of a SC manager is to guarantee the correct flows of goods and information throughout the SC nodes to ensure the right goods are at the right place at the right time.

1

Preliminaries in Decision-Making

1.1. Introduction

Supply chain (SC) is the framework that gathers different commercial entities perceived to be effective in the planning operations and cost-saving activities. We try in the present chapter to define the main concepts used within the SC and that are related to the decision-making between some entities of the SC, which is generally viewed as a course of actions to be handled and scheduled by the manager. The decision-making process starts by defining and stating the problem. Then, the problem designer should be able to depict the problem features that characterize the above-mentioned statements in order to select the appropriate solution approach. As illustrated in Figure 1.1, two main categories of solution approach exist: optimization approach and game theory approach. Once the solution approach is selected, it has to be evaluated by the use of specifically designed metrics. Simulations are then conducted in order to produce comparative study of the solution approach.

Hence, the decision-making process is decomposed into elementary steps to be handled by appropriate experts and validated to measure the real gap between the theoretical plan and its implementation. This system realization, implementation and validation makes its design (from a theoretical point of view) and building (from a practical standpoint) more coherent and much more efficient once compared to the initial problem specification and system concept that can be pointed out from the following list:

1) *System*: a set of components intercorrelated by precedence and resource requirements in order to accomplish one or several objectives.

2) *Closed system*: a system that does not need any external interaction to accomplish its objective(s).

3) *Open system*: a system that continuously needs external interactions to accomplish its objective(s).

4) *Suboptimality*: the quality of the solution related to the accomplishment of the system objective(s) and to be the best, in which case it is called "optimal", or close to the best, in which case it is called "suboptimal". The quality of such a solution is closely dependent on the complexity of the process.

Once the decision-making process is defined and clearly specified, the problem should be analyzed and quantitatively expressed in terms of its inputs and outputs.

The remainder of this chapter is organized as follows. In section 1.2, we define the decision-making problems. Section 1.3 deals with the optimization modeling of the decision problem. Section 1.4 presents the game theory modeling for the decision-making problems.

1.2. Decision-making problems

A decision-making problem is the quantitative modeling of a problem situation. Generally speaking, a decision-making problem is split into the following three main components:

– the decision maker(s);

– the objective(s) to be reached;

– the set of structural constraints (system constraints and decision variables) that bound the feasible set.

Depending on these components, we can point out the solution approaches that solve a decision-making problem. To do so, it is required for the decision maker (DM) to study the problem complexity in order to identitfy the class to which the deicison problem lies. We can point out two main solution approaches for a decision problem: the optimization or the game theory approach.

For the optimization modeling, two main classes of decision-making problems are:

1) *Constrained decision problems* modeled as the optimization of an objective function $z(x)$ expressed while fulfilling a set of structural constraints that bound the decision space. So, three components can characterize a constrained decision problem, namely, the objective function, the set of constraints and the decision variable requirements.

2) *Unconstrained decision problems* that consist of minimizing or maximizing a function $z(x)$ that is generally nonlinear. The main concern is the finding of the

solution value that corresponds to the local optima of $z(x)$. In this case, there is neither consideration of system constraints nor of the range of the solution x.

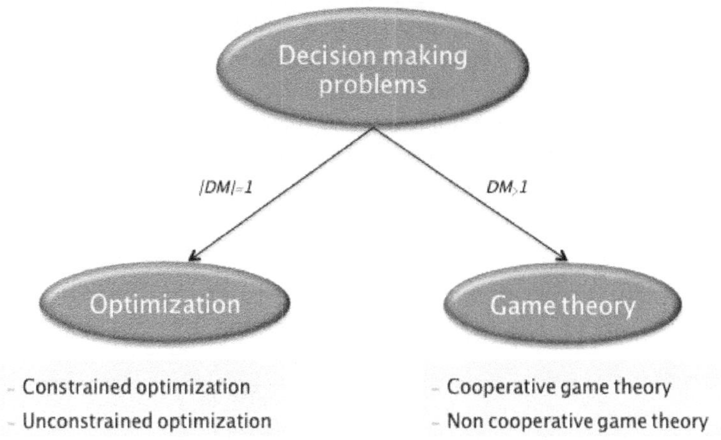

Figure 1.1. *Taxonomy of decision-making problems*

From a game theoretical standpoint, we point out two main classes:

1) *cooperative games* that model a collaborative decision-making process where a group of players (decision makers) can coordinate their actions and share their winnings. In fact, the cooperative game theory deals with how players can synchronize their decisions and divide the spoils after they have made binding agreements;

2) *non-cooperative games* that address the problem with multiple decision makers where each one has to choose among various options from several possible choices. However, the preferences that each decision maker has on his actions depend on the actions of the others. Thus, his action depends on his beliefs about what the others are willing to do. The main idea of non-cooperative game theory is thus to analyze and understand such a multi-person decision-making process.

1.3. Optimization modeling of a decision problem

An optimization problem is a formal specification of a set of proposals related to a specific framework that includes one decision maker, one or several objectives to be reached and a set of structural constraints. A possible structure of an optimization modeling is shown in Figure 1.2. Optimization has been practiced in numerous fields of study as it provides a primary tool for modeling and solving complex and hard constrained problems. Throughout the 1960s, integer programming formulations and approximate approaches received considerable attention as useful tools in solving optimization problems. Depending on the problem structure and its complexity, appropriate solution approaches were proposed to generate appropriate solutions in a reasonable computation time. Several optimization studies are formulated as a problem whose goal is to find the best solution, which corresponds to the minimum or maximum value of a single objective function. The challenge of solving combinatorial problems lies in their computational complexity since most of them are NP-hard [GAR 79]. This complexity can mainly be expressed in terms of the relationship between the search space and the difficulty to find a solution. The search space in combinatorial optimization problems is discrete and multidimensional. The dimensionality of the search space greatly influences the complexity of the decision problem.

Objective	$Min/Max \quad Z(x)$
Structural constraints	$g_1(x) \leq b_1$ $g_2(x) \leq b_2$ $\vdots$ $g_m(x) \leq b_m$
Decision variables	$x_1 \in A_1,\ x_2 \in A_2,\ \ldots,\ x_n \in A_n$

Figure 1.2. *Structure of an optimization problem*

1.3.1. *Notation*

We list below the major symbols used for defining an optimization problem:

Symbols	Description
n	the number of decision variables
k	the number of objectives
$x = (x_1, \ldots, x_n)^T$	the vector of decision variables
$c_{(p,n)}$	the cost matrix
A	the matrix of constraints
B	resource limitations
E_O	the set of efficient solutions in the objective space
E_D	the set of efficient solutions in the decision space

Assuming the linearity of an optimization problem, its mathematical modeling is outlined as follows:

$$Max\ p.x \qquad [1.1]$$

$$S.t.\ A.x \leq B \qquad [1.2]$$

$$x \in \mathcal{X} \qquad [1.3]$$

where $x = (x_1, \ldots, x_n)^T$ denotes the vector of decision variables, p, b and A are the constant vectors and matrix of coefficients, respectively.

Many variants of this formulation can be pointed out:

– *Continuous linear programming (CLP)*: the optimization model [1.1]–[1.3] is a CLP if the decision variables are continuous. For continuous linear optimization problems, efficient exact algorithms such as the simplex-type method [BÜR 12] or interior point methods exist [ANS 12].

– *Integer linear programming (ILP)*: the optimization model [1.1]–[1.3] is an ILP if $\mathcal{X}$ is the set of feasible integer solutions (i.e. decision variables are discrete). This class of models is very important as many real-life applications are modeled with discrete variables since their handled resources are indivisible (such as cars, machines and containers). A large number of combinatorial optimization problems can be formulated as ILPs (e.g. packing problems, scheduling problems and traveling salesman) in which the decision variables are discrete and the search space is finite. However, the objective function and constraints may take any form [PAP 82].

– *Mixed integer programming (MIP)*: the optimization model [1.1]–[1.4] is called MIP, when the decision variables are both discrete and continuous. Consequently, MIP models generalize CLP and ILP models. MIP problems have improved dramatically of late with the use of advanced optimization techniques such as relaxations and decomposition approaches, branch and bound and cutting plane algorithms when the problem sizes are small [GAR 11, WAN 14, COO 11]. Metaheuristics are also a good candidate for larger instances. They can also be used to generate good lower or upper bounds for exact algorithms and improve their efficiency.

1.3.2. *Features of an optimization problem*

Optimization problems can be classified in terms of the nature of the objective function and the nature of the constraints. Special forms of the objective function and the constraints give rise to specialized models that can efficiently model the problem under study. From this point of view, various types of optimization models can be highlighted: linear and nonlinear, single and multiobjective optimization problems and continuous and combinatorial programming models. Based on such features, we have to define the following points:

– *The number of decision makers:* if one DM is involved, the problem dealt with is an *optimization problem.* Otherwise, we are concerned with a *game* that can be cooperative or non-cooperative, depending on the DMs' standpoints.

– *The number of objectives*: this determines the nature of the solution to be generated. If only one objective is addressed in the decision problem, the best solution corresponds to the optimal solution. However, if more than one objective is considered, we are concerned with generating a set of efficient solutions that correspond to some tradeoffs between the objectives under study.

– *The linearity:* when both the objective(s) and the constraints are linear, the optimization problem is said to be linear. In this case, specific solution approaches can be adapted as the simplex method. Otherwise, the problem is nonlinear, in which case the resolution becomes more complex and the decision space is not convex.

– *The nature of the decision variables:* if the decision variables are integer, we deal with a combinatorial optimization problem.

1.3.3. *A didactic example*

Let us consider the following optimization problem involving two decision variables x_1 and x_2. We show in this illustrative example, inspired from [KRI 14a], how the solution changes in terms of the nature of the decision variables that can be either continuous or binary and the number of objectives $k = 1, 2$. Hence, four optimization problems follow:

	SINGLE OBJECTIVE	MULTI-OBJECTIVE
CONTINUOUS DECISION VARIABLES	$\begin{array}{ll} Max & 2x_1 + x_2 \\ S.t. & 5x_1 + 7x_2 \leq 100 \\ & x_1 - 3x_2 \leq 80 \\ & x \geq 0 \end{array} \Rightarrow \boxed{\begin{array}{l}(x_1, x_2) = (20, 0) \\ z(x) = 40\end{array}}$	$\begin{array}{ll} Max & 2x_1 + x_2 \\ & x_1 + 5x_2 \\ S.t. & 5x_1 + 7x_2 \leq 100 \\ & x_1 - 3x_2 \leq 80 \\ & x \geq 0 \end{array}$ $\Downarrow$ $\boxed{\begin{array}{l} E_D = \{(20, 0), (0, 14.285)\} \\ E_O = \{\begin{pmatrix} 40 \\ 20 \end{pmatrix} \begin{pmatrix} 14.285 \\ 71.428 \end{pmatrix}\} \end{array}}$
BINARY DECISION VARIABLES	$\begin{array}{ll} Max & 2x_1 + x_2 \\ S.t. & 5x_1 + 7x_2 \leq 100 \\ & x_1 - 3x_2 \leq 80 \\ & x \in \{0, 1\} \end{array} \Rightarrow \boxed{\begin{array}{l}(x_1, x_2) = (1, 1) \\ z(x) = 3\end{array}}$	$\begin{array}{ll} Max & 2x_1 + x_2 \\ & x_1 + 5x_2 \\ S.t. & 5x_1 + 7x_2 \leq 100 \\ & x_1 - 3x_2 \leq 80 \\ & x \in \{0, 1\} \end{array}$ $\Downarrow$ $\boxed{\begin{array}{l} E_D = \{(1, 1)\} \\ E_O = \{\begin{pmatrix} 3 \\ 6 \end{pmatrix}\} \end{array}}$

As mentioned previously, the resolution of the single objective optimization problem yields to the finding of the optimal solution that varies depending on the nature of the decision variables. However, if a second objective is added, the resolution generates a set of Pareto-optimal solutions, as it is the case for $k = 2$.

1.4. Game theory modeling of a decision problem

Game theory has become an important tool in the decision-making areas. Indeed, it is considered as an alternative way that achieves cost-saving objectives. These are realized using various collaboration schemas. Such schemas try to form coalitions of players in order to minimize or maximize a given objective. The coalition formation problem (CFP) covers two fundamental behavioral social notions: conflict (competition) and cooperation. As such, the theory of games was divided into two distinct types: non-cooperative game theory and cooperative game theory. In the non-cooperative theory, a game is a detailed model of all the moves available to the players. However, the preferences that each decision maker has on his actions depend on the actions of the others. By contrast, cooperative theory abstracts away from this level of detail, and only describes the outcomes that result when the players come together in different combinations [BRA 07]. Once the type of game theory is defined, the decision of each player to join the coalition or not is based on its shared payoff generated due to that coalition formation regarding its individual payoff. This shared payoff is calculated using an allocation method. The main objective of the game theory is to find a stable coalition structure where no player has an interest in deviating from the coalition.

1.4.1. *Notation*

We list below the major symbols used for defining a game theoretical problem:

Symbols	Description
$v(S)$	the payoff function
n	the number of players
S	the subset of coalitions
$N = \{1, 2, ..., n\}$	the set of players
i	the player's index

Theoretical games can be defined as a set of n players/participants that can coordinate their objectives and synchronize their strategies in order to achieve cost saving while sharing information and allocating payoffs.

Let $N = \{1, 2, ..., n\}$ be a finite set of players with different cooperation possibilities. Each subset $S \in N$ is referred to each formed coalition or alliance. We recall that a coalition is the group of players that synchronize their strategies and goals. The number of coalitions is $2^n - 1$. For each S, $\|S\|$ refers to the number of agents within the coalition. $v(S)$ be the characteristic function that associates a real number with each coalition S which can be interpreted as the maximum value of cost savings that the members of S would divide among themselves. Given a coalition S, we define an allocation: $(x_1, x_2, ..., x_n)$ as a division of the overall created value. It specifies for each player $i \in S$ the payoff portion x_i that this player will receive when he cooperates with other players. We give in what follows some features of an allocation:

– an allocation $(x_1, x_2, ..., x_n)$ is *individually rational* if $x_i \geq v(i)$ for all i;

– an allocation $(x_1, x_2, ..., x_n)$ is efficient if $\sum_{i=1}^{\|N\|} x(i) = v(N)$;

– *an imputation* is an efficient and individually rational allocation;

– *a stability* of a coalition structure is given if $\sum_{i \in S} x_i \leq v(S)$.

The individual rationality means that a division of the overall value (i.e. an allocation) must give each player as much value as that player receives without interacting with other players (single coalition). Efficiency means that all the value that can be created can, in fact, be divided among collaborating players.

1.4.2. *The coalition formation problem*

The CFP models many situations in multiple domains including multi-agent systems, economics, industry or politics. One approach is concerned with cases where a group of players is interested in accomplishing, individually or cooperatively, one common task. The other is interested in sets of autonomous, self-motivated players who act in order to achieve their own task or increase their own profit. A solution to the CFP consists of:

– dispatching the players into coalitions forming a "coalition structure". This step is called the coalition structure generation (CSG). This step tries to search for the coalition structure corresponding to the maximum total sum of coalition values;

– dividing the gains among the players in such a way that no player is tempted to deviate. This is called the payoff division (PD).

Game theorists modeled the CFP as a cooperative game in its two forms, either as a characteristic function game or as a partition function game, in order to obtain stable payoff vectors [STE 68] and [KAH 84]. However, game theory did not provide any mechanism to form coalitions of the players.

Games with externalities assume that the payoff of a coalition depends on what other coalitions form [BLO 96]. A function assigning to each coalition a payoff depending on the whole coalition structure is called a "partition function". Such a game is called a "partition function game" [MAR 03].

All created works addressed the CFP in terms of two main features: the superadditivity and the non-superadditivity. A game is superadditive if each two subgroups of players receive at least as much when cooperating as by acting individually. Therefore, the CSG step will obviously generate the grand coalition.

Table 1.1 reports the main research that has addressed the CFP. These works are concerned in solving either the CSG step or the PD step. We continue this research by addressing both features of the problem (CSG and PD) mainly for non-superadditive games.

	Superadditive games	*Non-superadditive games*
CSG	*The grand coalition forms in all cases*	[DAN 04], [SAN 99] [SEN 00] [YAN 07] [LAR 00]
PD	[STE 68] [KAH 84] [BEL 06] [GIL 59] [AUM 74] [SHA 53] Hart (1997)	[YAN 07]

Table 1.1. *Classification of the CF papers in terms of the superadditivity*

When the game is not superadditive, the proposed approaches try to generate the coalition structures that maximize the total welfare as in [YAN 07], without dividing the obtained payoff among the players.

The PD was addressed mainly for superadditive games. Various stability concepts were proposed in the literature to define a dividing strategy with two alternative designs:

1) non-cooperative game: prisoner's dilemma "Nash equilibrium" *Pollute, Risk*;

2) cooperative game: coalition formation... "Nash equilibrium, Shapley, Core" *Profit, Cost*.

The payoff vector x should fulfill the following rationality concepts. To do so, let N be a set of players, $S \subseteq N$ a coalition of players, CS a coalition structure and C the set of all coalition structures of N.

1) *Individual rationality*: a payoff vector $x = (x_1, .., x_n)$ is said to be individually rational if it satisfies:

$$x_i \geq v(\{i\}) \quad \forall i \in N \qquad [1.4]$$

2) *Coalitional rationality*: a payoff vector $x = (x_1, .., x_n)$ is said to be coalitionally rational if it satisfies:

$$\sum_{i \in S} x_i \geq v(S) \quad \forall S \subseteq N \qquad [1.5]$$

3) *Efficiency*: an efficient payoff vector $x = (x_1, .., x_n)$ for non-superadditive games can be written as:

$$\sum_{i \in N} x_i = \max_{CS \in C} \sum_{S \in CS} v(S) \qquad [1.6]$$

1.4.3. *The stability concepts*

Nash equilibrium: this is a fundamental concept in the theory of games and the most widely used method of predicting the outcome of strategic interaction in the social sciences. A game consists of the following three elements: a set of players, a set of actions available to each player and a payoff (or utility) function for each player. The payoff functions represent each player's preferences over action profiles, where an action profile is simply a list of actions, one for each player. A pure-strategy Nash equilibrium is an action profile with the property that no single player can obtain a higher payoff by deviating unilaterally from this profile.

Core stability: to define the core, some additional notations will be useful. For any subset S of the set of players N, let $x(S) = \sum_{i \in S} x(i)$. In other words, the term $x(S)$ denotes the sum of the values received by each of the players i in the subset S.

DEFINITION 1.1 AN ALLOCATION.– $(x_1, x_2, ..., x_n)$ is *collectively rational* if $x(S) \geq v(S)$ for all i.

DEFINITION 1.2 THE CORE.– [SHA 53] This is the set of efficient allocations satisfying the collective rationality.

$$Cr(N, v) = \{x(N) = v(N) and x(S) \geq v(S)\} \qquad [1.7]$$

In a game (N, v), if any group of players, say S, anticipated capturing a lower value in total than the group could create on its own, i.e. if $x(S) < v(S)$, then this group of players would do better to create a coalition apart, S, and divide the value $v(S)$ by themselves. This would not happen under core allocations. In summary, the core has the interesting interpretation that the total created value is allocated in such a way that no group of players would have the incentive to leave the system (the grand coalition N) and form a coalition apart because they collectively receive at least as much value as they could obtain for themselves as a coalition. The grand coalition is then immune to coalitional deviations, this concept has been called the core stability.

DEFINITION 1.3 THE GRAND COALITION N.– This is said to be stable or core stable if it has a non-empty core.

1.5. Allocation methods

In this section, we turn our attention to describing the three allocation rules that we use in the rest of the dissertation. This includes equal allocations, proportional allocations and Shapley value allocations.

1.5.1. *Shapley value allocation*

This section is devoted to introducing the concepts and axioms of Shapley value [SHA 53], one of the most central solution concepts in game theory. Shapley value is a solution that prescribes a single payoff for each player, which is the average of all marginal contributions of that player to each coalition of which he is a member. It satisfies the following axioms:

– efficiency: the payoffs must add up to $v(N)$, which means that all the grand coalition surplus is allocated;

– symmetry: if two players are substitutable because they contribute the same to each coalition, the solution should treat them equally;

– additivity: the solution to the sum of two games must be the sum of what it awards to each of the two games;

– dummy player: if a player contributes nothing to every coalition, the solution should pay him nothing.

There is a unique single-valued solution to games satisfying efficiency, symmetry, additivity and dummy. The function that assigns to each player i the payoff [SHA 53]:

$$Sh(N,v)(i) = \sum_{i \in S} \frac{(\|S\| - 1)! - (\|N\| - \|S\|!)}{\|N\|!} (v(s) - v(s\|i)) \qquad [1.8]$$

The Shapley value awards to each player the average of his marginal contributions to each coalition. The marginal contribution of a player i with respect to a given ordering is defined as his marginal worth to the players before him in the order, $v(1, 2, ..., i-1, i) - v(1, 2, ..., i-1)$ where $1, , i-1$ are the players preceding i in the given ordering. The Shapley value is obtained by averaging the marginal contributions for all possible orderings. In taking this average, all orders of the players are considered to be equally likely.

The Shapley value is usually viewed as a good normative answer to the question posed in cooperative game theory, that is, those who contribute more to the groups that they belong to should be paid more. However, the Shapley value may be not stable in the sense of the core. For instance, it may allocate a negative value to some players. Besides, the Shapley value may lie outside the core unless for some special games like convex games [SHA 71]. For a recent study on Shapley value's stability, see [BEA 08].

Equal allocations: the simplest allocation of savings would be to give an equal portion to each player.

$$v(i) = \frac{v(N)}{n} \qquad [1.9]$$

Proportional allocation: another simple way of allocating savings would be to distribute them proportionally to the initial inputs (contributions) of different players. For example, consider a savings game (N, v) such that $v(S) = (\sum_{i \in S} C(i)/C(S))$ for any coalition S, the function C is the cost characteristic function. The savings may be allocated proportionally to the stand-alone cost (individual cost) of each player. This devision protocol is termed the cost-based proportional rule. Each player i gets,

$$v(i) = \frac{v(i)}{\sum_{j \in S} v(j)} v(N) \qquad [1.10]$$

1.6. Conclusion

We outlined in this chapter the main concepts related to the decision-making process. As such, we pointed out two main classes of decision-making problems, in terms of the number of involed DMs. For the single DM we surveyed the most important tools that characterize the resolution of such a class seen as an optimization problem that can address one or multiple objectives subject to structural constraints. The resolution of an optimization problem depends on numerous features mainly the complexity of the problem and its size. Alternatively, if multiple DMs are involved in the decision problem, the problem modeling corresponds to a game that can be cooperative or non-cooperative, depending on players' standpoints. We discussed some stability concepts related to game theory. We also detailed, for cooperative games, the need for a coalition formation and the incentive of forming coalitions followed by numerous payoff division protocols. All such concepts will be used in the subsequent chapters that focus on supply chain activities involving single or multiple DMS.

2

Introduction to Supply Chain Management

2.1. Introduction

Supply chain management (SCM) is the decision-making process that manages different activities that generate advantageous profits to the suppliers, retailers and customers involved. In addition, the efficient planning of activities can be profitable for product development, sourcing, production, logistics and all flows that can link those activities. SCM can also be seen as the process of optimizing a set of decisions that generate cost-effective solutions which provide efficient plans for acting on numerous levels while taking into account all decision-making standpoints.

SCM can therefore be defined as the set of activities utilized to efficiently integrate the different elements of the supply chain (SC), which involve suppliers, retailers and customers, so that products are produced and distributed at the right quantities, to the right locations and at the right time, in order to maximize system gain while satisfying service-level requirements.

The remainder of this chapter is organized as follows. In section 2.2, we define the main elements in the SC, section 2.3 defines the main activities in the SC and section 2.4 outlines the decision levels in the SCM.

2.2. Main elements of the supply chain

The efficiency and the performance of the SC are defined by the needs of each entity involved in the supply network, to lower its costs and increase its productivity. These needs depend on the way each entity builds and operates its supply functions.

Figure 2.1 presents an SC as a distribution network of all entities and functions, involved in moving a product from the supplier to the retailer, through warehouses to eventually end with the customer. A typical network may involve a variety of functions in order to fulfill a customer's demands. Every function fits into one or more SC entities and has a role to play in each of them. Therefore, the concept of SCM is mainly based on cumulative effort of all entities to optimize such functions and to reach, efficiently, an end customer. SCM, therefore, is the active management of SC functions to maximize customer value and achieve a sustainable competitive advantage whilst staying cost-effective. It represents a conscious effort by all entities to develop and execute SCs in the most effective possible ways. Figure 2.1 outlines the main activities that may be accomplished within the SC, such as the ordering, the warehousing, the inventory and the delivery. It is important to note that an effective management of SC activities highly contributes to the minimization of the cost incurred by the SC entities. Entities in an SC are defined as decision makers that manage the four functions previously described. In Figure 2.1, the three relevant entities that constitute the SC are detailed.

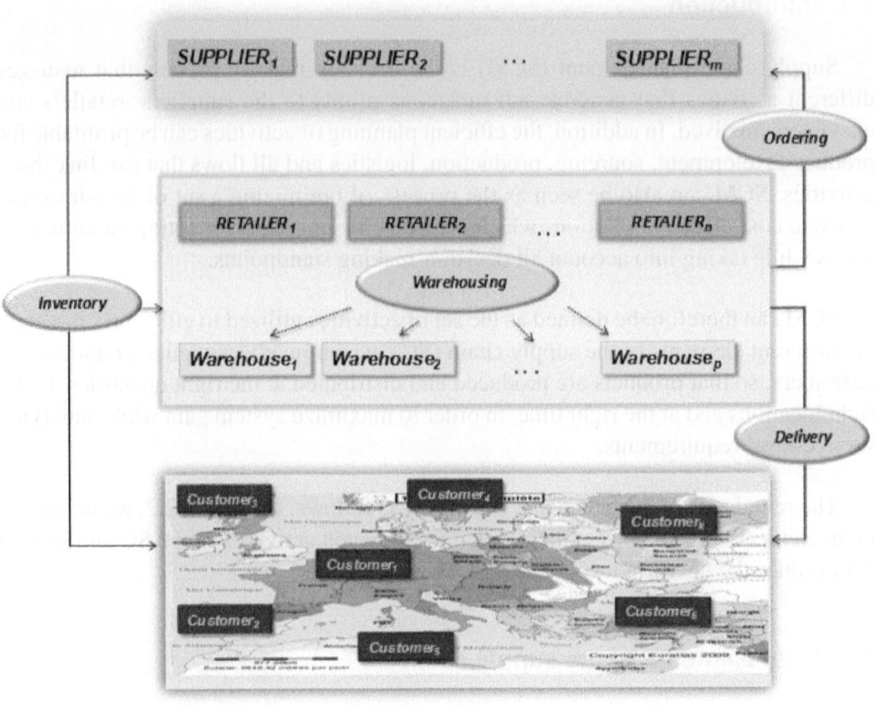

Figure 2.1. *Supply chain structure*

1) *Suppliers:* the suppliers are the organizations that produce finished products. They use the raw materials made by other producers to create their private products. Two types of products are defined: intangible items, such as music, software, service and designs, and tangible items, such as industrial products. Here, we focus on the second categories of tangible products.

2) *Retailers:* the retailers are the entities that stock inventory and sell in small quantities to the final customers. The main role of the retailers is to satisfy the customers' needs in an optimal way. In fact, they propose to their customers a combination of products, prices and services. Each retailer locates a set of private warehouses to stock products in order to respond to customers' needs without delay.

3) *Customers:* design the organizations that sell and use a product. A customer may purchase a product either to incorporate it to another customer or to consume it (also called consumers).

The first layer of the SC corresponds to the set of suppliers that provide items, which can be either raw materials or finished products. Each supplier disposes of its own selling policy that generally consists of proposing:

– A price p_j that does not depend on the quantity q to be ordered

In this case, only one price is considered. Hence, the selling volume of each supplier j:

$$c_j = p_j \times q, \ \ \forall q \in IN \qquad [2.1]$$

Subsequently, the set of suppliers is characterized by the following purchasing costs, given a quantity q to be ordered:

$$\left.\begin{array}{l} \boldsymbol{Supplier_1} \Rightarrow c_1 = p_1 \times q \\ \boldsymbol{Supplier_2} \Rightarrow c_p = p_2 \times q \\ \quad\vdots \\ \boldsymbol{Supplier_m} \Rightarrow c_m = p_m \times q \end{array}\right\} \textit{Each supplier should adjust its price}$$

Based on such computations, each supplier j should adjust its c_j in order to maximize its total profit issued by one of the following two parameters, or both:

- *the unit profit* (p_j): the margin of profit is high so that even if the ordered quantity is low, the total profit is high,

- *the quantity* (q): the margin of profit is low in which case the total profit is high due to the ordered quantity.

In summary, it is noticeable that if the price offered by the supplier is independent of the ordered quantity, there is no need for coalition formation.

EXAMPLE 2.1.– *An example of a one shot purchasing price*

Let us consider a $(2, 3)$-sized SC that involves a set of $m = 2$ suppliers and $n = 3$ retailers.

$$\left.\begin{array}{l} \textbf{Supplier}_1 \Rightarrow c_1 = 1 \times q \\ \textbf{Supplier}_2 \Rightarrow c_p = 2 \times q \end{array}\right\} \textit{Supplier}_2 \textit{ should adjust his price}$$

$$\Downarrow$$

$$\textit{Supplier}_1$$

The most advantageous purchasing price is c_1. Consequently, $supplier1$ will revise its pricing policy regarding the proposed prices in the market. In fact, the low price of $supplier_1$ enhances retailers to order considerable quantities in such a way that the profit will be generated in terms of the ordered quantity even if the unit profit is low.

In this case, the 3 retailers will order from $supplier_1$. Furthermore, there is no need for coalition formation as cumulative orders do not generate any additional benefit.

Let us assume that retailers' orders are the following:

Retailer	1	2	3
Quantity	30	100	50

In this case, $supplier_1$ will realize a selling volume of:

$$Selling = 1 \times (30 + 100 + 50) = 180^{DT} \quad [2.2]$$

Indeed, each supplier will order individually.

– *A quantity-dependent price* p_j

Suppliers can alternatively propose prices that depend on the ordered quantities in the sense that the selling volume of each supplier j decreases if the ordered quantity exceeds a prefixed threshold of the ordered quantities. In other words, each supplier j tries to offer a quantity discount e_j and an initial unit cost c_j. For a threshold quantity Q_{max}, suppliers deliver the ordered quantities with a minimal cost of C_{min} that entices retailers to order larger quantities than their economic-order quantity. Hence, the general purchasing cost with discount is reported as follows:

$$c_j = \begin{cases} p_j & \text{if } q = 0 \\ p_j - e_j \times q & \text{if } 0 < q < Q_{max} \\ C_{min} & \text{if } q \geq Q_{max} \end{cases} \qquad [2.3]$$

where: Q_{max} is expressed as:

$$Q_{max} = \frac{p_j - C_{min}}{e_j} \qquad [2.4]$$

EXAMPLE 2.2.– *An example of a one shot purchasing price*

Let us consider a $(1, 3)$-sized SC that involves a set of $m = 1$ suppliers and $n = 3$ retailers. The purchasing cost is expressed as follows:

$$c_j = \begin{cases} 50 & \text{if } q = 0 \\ 50 - 0.005 \times q & \text{if } 0 < q < Q_{max} \\ 43.5 & \text{if } q \geq Q_{max} \end{cases}$$

where

$$Q_{max} = \frac{50 - 43.5}{0.005} = 1300$$

Let us assume that retailers' orders are the following:

Retailer	1	2	3
Quantity	500	400	400

Based on such proposed purchasing function, supplier j should adjust its c_j in order to maximize its total profit according to the retailers ordering strategies that differ in the tasks to be handled either individually or by forming coalitions:

– *The stand-alone strategy*: each retailer is acting individually to demand its orders from the supplier. In such a case, supplier j will realize a selling volume of:

$$Selling = (500 \times 47.5 + 400 \times 48 + 400 \times 48) = 62.150^{DT} \qquad [2.5]$$

as the ordered quantity of each retailer belongs in the second landing of the purchasing function;

– *The collaborative strategy*: retailers have the possibility of joining their orders to benefit from the discount proposed by the supplier. Consequently, the selling volumes according to the possible coalition structures are the following:

- {1,2};{3}: Selling = $(900 \times 45.5 + 400 \times 48) = 60.150DT$,

- {1,3};{3}: Selling = $(900 \times 45.5 + 400 \times 48) = 60.150DT$,

- {2,3};{1}: Selling = $(800 \times 46 + 500 \times 47.5) = 60.550DT$,

- {1,2,3}: Selling = $(1300 \times 43.5) = 56.550DT$.

In the following section, we detail all activities presented in Figure 2.1.

2.3. Main activities in the supply chain

2.3.1. *The ordering problem*

The ordering of items is an activity that involves a set of retailers and a set of suppliers. It is generally labeled as a (n, m)-ordering problem that, depending on the number of suppliers, can require a supplier selection step. Based on the decomposition reported in Table 2.1, the main features that can determine the ordering problems structure are:

1) The cardinality of the set of retailers 1 or n $\quad$ [2 *possibilities*]

2) The cardinality of the set of suppliers 1 or m $\quad$ [2 *possibilities*]

3) The purchasing price policy that can be $\begin{cases} fixed & [2\ possibilities] \\ quantity - dependent \end{cases}$

$\overline{\qquad\qquad}$

6 *possibilities*

These features give rise to six variants of the problem that differ in the tasks to be handled either individually or by forming coalitions, in order to minimize the total ordering cost. Hence, the ordering problem consists, generally, of a subset of the following set of steps:

– supplier selection;

– collaboration;

– order launching.

Price/cardianlity	$(1, 1)$	$(n, 1)$	$(1, m)$	(n, m)
Fixed	– Order launching	– Order launching	– Supplier selection – Order launching	– Supplier selection – Order launching
Quantity dependent	– Order launching	– Collaboration	– Supplier selection	– Supplier selection – Collaboration – Order launching

Table 2.1. *Main variants of the ordering problem*

2.3.2. *The warehousing problem*

One of the main challenges of the retailers in the SC is the storage of ordered items in available warehouses that can be used either individually or by sharing the storage cost. We point out two main classes of warehousing problems (Figure 2.2):

– variable cost warehousing problem;

– fixed cost warehousing problem.

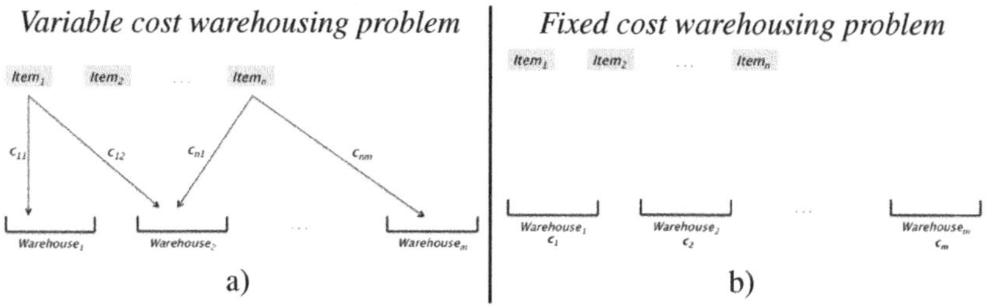

Figure 2.2. *Main classes of warehousing problems*

The warehousing problem, in its basic version, consists of selecting a minimum number of identical warehouses in order to load a set of products, given their weights and values. Several constraints, as variable bins' capacities and warehouses' compatibilities, can be added to the warehousing problem giving rise to many variants that model real case studies. In other words, given a number of private warehouses and facing various customers' demands, the retailer aims to find the best warehousing strategy that minimizes the number of used warehouses and the overall warehousing costs. Figure 2.3 is an illustration of warehousing problem.

2.3.3. *The transportation problem*

In the area of SCM, transportation problems are related to determining optimal routes for vehicles going from one or more distribution centers to a set of customer locations. These problems are known as vehicle routing problems (VRPs) and have a fundamental economic importance in the field of distribution and SCM. The main objective of the VRP is to deliver a set of customers with known demands while minimizing the transportation costs and respecting the delivery time expected by the customer. Hence, the VRP consists of finding a set of routes for K identical vehicles starting and ending at the distribution center. By involving additional constraints and requirements on routes construction, various VRP variants are to be defined. The capacitated VRP (CVRP) is the most addressed version that involves a fleet of vehicles specified by a weight capacity. The VRP with time windows (VRPTW), imposing a prefixed threshold of delivery time, should satisfy customers' requirements. The VRP with pick-up and delivery (PDP) differs from the classical VRP in the sense that goods have to be picked-up and delivered in specific amounts in the routes. Finally, the heterogeneous fleet VRP (HVRP) is characterized by different capacities for the set of vehicles.

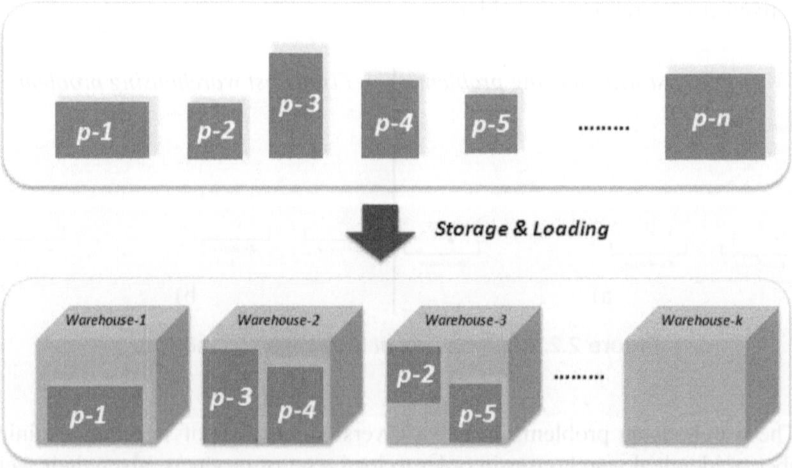

Figure 2.3. *An illustration of the warehousing problem*

2.3.4. *The inventory problem*

A challenging problem that involves the three main entities of the SC (suppliers, retailers and customers) is the inventory problem whose solution begins with an in-depth study of customers' demands for the appropriate quantities to be ordered while taking into account the quantities that exist in the corresponding warehouses. Hence, we can sum up the inventory management problem to be a master problem that can be handled in terms of ordering, warehousing and transportation problems' outputs. In fact, the inventory management problem within the SC plays a critical role because it strongly affects the SC performances. Lee [LEE 93] considered inventory control as the only tool to ensure SC stability, robustness and efficiency in the sense that the computation of all ordered elements is online with the stored quantities, customers' demands and the delivery cost. Regarding all such components, the inventory management problem positively affects the SC sustainability. Based on such concepts, the objective of SC inventory management is to satisfy the customer's demands by increasing the quality and service level while at the same time decreasing total costs. Inventories affect SC costs and performances in terms of:

– tied up values, raw materials have a lower value than finished products;

– degrees of flexibility, raw materials have higher flexibility than the finished products because they can be easily adopted for different production processes;

– levels of responsiveness, e.g. products delivery could be made without strict lead times, whereas raw material transformation usually requires stringent lead times.

However, the inventory problem is not the only critical issue affecting SC performance. The internal logistics management within each SC node (i.e. warehouse management in a distribution center) similarly affects SC performance. The correct organization of all the logistic processes and activities that take place within a SC node (i.e. capability of using material-handling systems efficiently, time windows planning for suppliers/retailers, unloading/loading operations, etc.) could have a remarkable impact on processes both upstream and downstream of the SC and on SC node internal costs.

The inventory management system at each SC node has to address the following three issues:

1) review the stock status;

2) define the appropriate time to order new products;

3) compute the quantity to be ordered.

2.3.5. *Computer science applications in supply chain management*

The recent economic environment is characterized by its expanded pressure for globalization and competitiveness. The latter has made exchanging information between involved entities within the SC a critical task that affects its performance. In fact, entities have to be adapted to new business models and rethink their role and position given the possibility of utilizing and exchanging big data in order to improve the SC performance. To do so, efforts have been made to create and organize central information system solutions. For instance, cloud-based information systems represent a better alternative to establish an information technology support for the SCM [SCH 12]. Such information support is mainly based on decision support systems (DSS) that provide a current market perspective on cloud computing and SC from the position of logistics and from the perspective of the software industry. This outlines the potentials of the DSS architectures to evaluate the SCM. Based on the above discussion, numerous computer science applications within the SC are to be pointed out:

1) *DSS implementation for handling SC activities*: the fast design of an electronic platform is less reliable in terms of individual expertise and skills for the decision-maker (DM). In fact, the DM is looking for a simple interface that can be easily and rapidly managed in order to provide appropriate deicsions. Furthermore, the DM is allowed to perform strategic analyses by viewing available information in a statistical way to determine minimal, maximal and average costs incurred by the firm per time period and assessing service and cost levels. Figure 2.4 illustrates the use of the DSS by the firm's manager in order to make strategic decisions related to the ordering and delivery of items [KRI 14b]

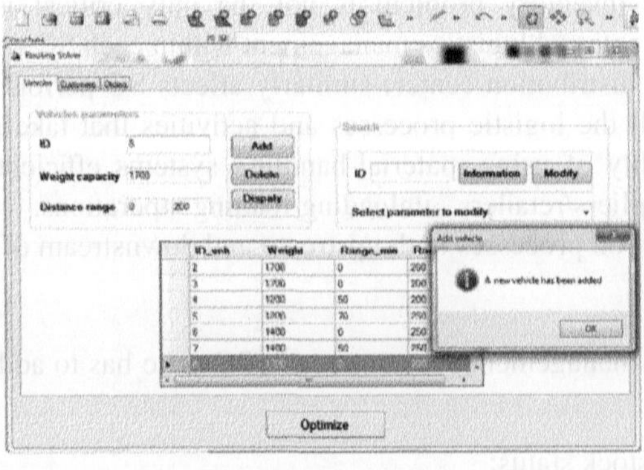

Figure 2.4. *A DSS for the SC activities: ordering and delivery*

2) *Cloud computing for SC information storage in virtual machines*: given large volumes of data, and for security reasons, it is highly recommended to use cloud computing to make sure that SC information is safe and reliable.

3) *Big data analytics*: firms in the SC try to adopt cost-effective tools to make right decisions during their survival in the market. Such studies address both *ad hoc* and specific situations. They also try to perform up-to-date tools that manage everyday decision making as well as sensitive decisions. For this purpose, processing large amounts of data, stored during the last years, quickly reaches its limits. Therefore, big data management is very helpful for a sustainable and efficient decision-making process.

2.4. Decision levels in the supply chain

In the SCM, the decisions can be classified into three levels: strategic, tactical and operational level. Each level is distinguished by the period of time over which decisions are made, and the granularity of decisions during that period.

2.4.1. *Strategic level*

Strategic decisions are typically made over a long time period. At the strategic level, each entity in the SC decides on the number, location and mission of the facilities to operate and selects the portfolio of suppliers to employ in order to design a value-creating supply network [KLI 10]. These are closely linked to the corporate strategy and guide SC policies from a design perspective. Strategic decisions may also include the decisions related to information and technology infrastructure that support the SC operations, and to strategic partnership.

2.4.2. *Tactical level*

When the supply network is designed by the entity and becomes operational, it is managed to respond, on a tactical and operational basis, to customers' demands through planning and control processes. Tactical (or mid-term) decisions include planning decisions aimed at balancing charge and capacity. Such decisions include the production (contracting, locations, scheduling and planning process definition), inventory (quantity, location and quantity of inventory), sourcing contracts and other purchasing decisions.

2.4.3. *Operational level*

Finally, the operational decision level addresses issues such as inventory deployment, detailed scheduling and daily shipment. The so-called "flow management" level is relative to short time decisions, such as the decisions of launching the production, ordering and transportation of orders.

2.5. Conclusion

This chapter outlines the main components that define the SC network, i.e. the entities and the activities within the SC. We began by giving a brief description of the different elements of the SC network. After that, we focused on the cooperative SC's activities. The last section of this chapter was devoted to the main supply decision levels. In Chapter 3, we will detail the ordering problem in the SCM.

3

The Ordering Problem

3.1. Introduction

Ordering refers to the forecasting of products, either for internal use or for distribution, to meet external end-customers needs. The ordering process consists of the following questions: what type of product will be ordered, how much is needed, and when and where will the products be needed. It also determines where and when to source products and how much inventory to carry. The management of the ordering function requires respecting of the logistic network and supply chain constraints, such as warehouse capacity, transport options and lead times. Many extensions to the ordering problem have been explored and differ by the number of levels in the supply chain and the number of actors at each level. Table 3.1 splits the ordering problem in terms of two main components, namely the number of suppliers (one or multiple) and the number of retailers (one or multiple). Hence, we address four problem types. For each type, the problem inputs are displayed and adapted in the following way:

$$(\underbrace{Fixed\ ordering\ cost,}_{a/a_j}\ \underbrace{Unit\ purshasing\ cost,}_{p/p_j}\ \underbrace{Retailer's\ demand,}_{d/d_i}$$
$$\underbrace{Unit\ holding\ cost)}_{h/h_i}$$

	One retailer	Multiple retailers
One supplier	$(a, p, d, h) \rightarrow EOQ$	$(a, p, d_i, h_i) \begin{cases} Collaboration \\ EOQ \end{cases}$
Multiple suppliers	$(a_j, p_j, d, h) \begin{cases} Supplier\ selection \\ EOQ \end{cases}$	$(a_j, p_j, d_i, h_i) \begin{cases} Supplier\ selection \\ Collaboration \\ EOQ \end{cases}$

Table 3.1. *Alternative ordering problems with respect to the supply chain taxonomy*

3.2. Terminology

The following symbols designate the shortcuts used for the ordering problem:

EOQ	The economic order quantity
TC	The total cost
PC	The purchasing cost
OC	The ordering cost
HC	The holding cost

where the total cost TC is expressed in terms of the purchasing cost, ordering cost and holding cost, as follows:

$$TC = PC + OC + HC \qquad [3.1]$$

We detail, in the following sections, each type of ordering problem and state the ordering process followed by the corresponding equations.

3.3. The one supplier–one retailer ordering problem

The one supplier/one retailer ordering problem is based on a distributed decision-making system having two hierarchical levels (e.g. between a supplier and a firm/firm or producer and supplier). It involves bargaining between the related decision-making units to achieve results that cannot be achieved by working in isolation [WAN 04]. Figure 3.1 presents a hierarchical link in a supply chain consisting of one supplier and one firm. In terms of hierarchical planning, the supplier represents the upper level whereas the firm represents the lower level in the decision-making process.

These two decision-making units are linked through connected flows of products and information belonging either at the strategic, tactical or operational level in the supply chain. However, at the strategic level, the overall design of the supply network is achieved [GEO 95], while at the tactical level we have the planning of the replenishment decisions that organize the concrete relationship between supply chain partners [TSA 99, CAC 99]. Finally, at the operational level, the current material and information flow are actually operated [HEN 97].

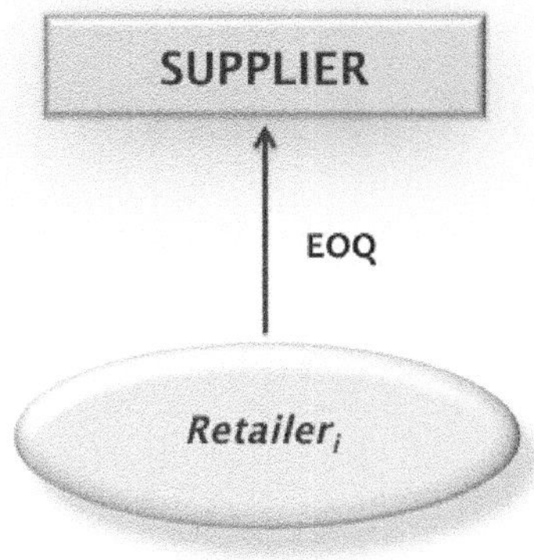

Figure 3.1. *A supply chain with one supplier and one retailer*

The objective of each firm is to decide how many units to order and when so as to maximize its total profit. Economic order quantity (EOQ) policy is viewed as a powerful model to achieve such an objective. This model is studied first owing to its simplicity and performance in considering the trade-off between purchasing, ordering and holding costs in choosing the quantity to use in replenishing good. Another advantage is that the model gives the optimal solution in closed form. This allows us to gain insights about the behavior of the system. The closed-form solution is also easy to compute. The EOQ is written as follows:

Inputs	*Outputs*
d: The annual demand quantity	q^*: The optimal order quantity
a: The fixed cost per order	m^*: The optimal number of orders
h: The unitary holding cost	
p: The unitary purchasing cost	

$$TC = \underbrace{pd}_{PC} + \underbrace{a\frac{d}{q}}_{OC} + \underbrace{h\frac{q}{2}}_{HC} \qquad [3.2]$$

In order to compute the EOQ that corresponds to the optimal quantity to be ordered, the more convenient way is to consider Q as the only variable in [5.2] and derive the optimal quantity to be addressed. To do so, we proceed to differentiate [5.2] and set it to 0, as reported in equation [5.3]:

$$0 = -\frac{da}{q^2} + \frac{h}{2} \quad [3.3]$$

Therefore, the EOQ is:

$$q^* = \sqrt{\frac{2da}{h}} \quad [3.4]$$

Consequently, the optimal number of periods is:

$$m^* = \frac{d}{q^*} \quad [3.5]$$

3.3.1. *An example of the one–one ordering problem*

Let us consider an ordering problem that involves one supplier and one retailer. The input data are reported in the first column of Table 3.2.

Inputs	*Outputs*
$d = 15000$	$q^* = \sqrt{\frac{2\times15000\times30}{10}} = 300$
$a = 30$	$m^* = \frac{15000}{300} = 50$
$h = 10$	
$p = 20$	

Table 3.2. *Inputs/outputs for a one supplier–one retailer ordering problem*

Based on the computations of equations [5.4] and [4.8], the optimal ordering policy is to launch 50 orders from the supplier. Each order amounts to 300 units. We can conduct, on this vein, a sensitivity analysis on the problem parameters and generate a tuning that can generate a desired threshold related to one of the involved components.

3.3.2. *Summary*

The one–one ordering problem can be stated in terms of the steps in Algorithm 1.

Algorithm 1: The one–one ordering problem

---

1. Input data

- Fixed ordering cost: a
- Purchasing cost: p
- Holding cost: h
- The total quantity to be ordered: d

2. Ordering process

1) Compute the EOQ

3. Output data

- q^*: the optimal quantity to be ordered at each period
- m^*: the optimal number of orders

3.4. The one supplier-multiple retailers ordering problem

An alternative design of the ordering process can address a set of retailers aiming to order from a single supplier. The ordering of items can be viewed as an incentive for all retailers to form coalitions in order to gather their orders for a cost-effective configuration. We address in what follows two supplier ordering policies:

1) *Fixed purchasing price*: the proposed supplier's price is independent of the ordered quantity.

2) *Quantity-dependent price*: the supplier proposes landings of prices in terms of the ordered quantity.

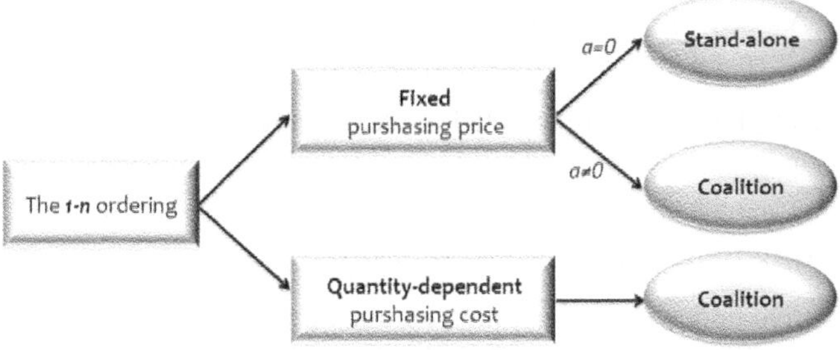

Figure 3.2. *Supply chain structure*

3.4.1. *Fixed purchasing price*

A fixed purchasing cost is modeled as predefined constant value "a" to be quantified at each ordering operation. The ordering cost for each retailer i ($i = 1, \dots, n$) is written as follows:

$$TC = p \times d_i + a\frac{d_i}{q_i} + h\frac{q_i}{2} \qquad [3.6]$$

When $\boldsymbol{a} = \mathbf{0}$, and because each retailer incurs its proper purchasing cost that depends only on the quantity to be ordered, there is no incentive for retailers to form coalitions for cost-saving finalities. Hence, the total cost for each retailer is:

$$TC = p \times d_i + h\frac{q_i}{2} \qquad [3.7]$$

3.4.2. *An example of the* $1 - n$ *ordering problem*

Let us consider an ordering problem that involves one supplier and $n = 3$ retailers. The input data are reported in the first column of Table 3.3.

Inputs	*Outputs*
$d_1 = 5000$	$q_1^* = \sqrt{\frac{2\times 5000\times 30}{10}} = 54.77$
$d_2 = 3000$	$q_2^* = \sqrt{\frac{2\times 3000\times 30}{10}} = 134.16$
$d_3 = 8000$	$q_3^* = \sqrt{\frac{2\times 8000\times 30}{10}} = 219.08$
$a = 30$	$m^* = \frac{15000}{300} = 50$
$h = 10$	
$p = 20$	

Table 3.3. *Inputs/outputs for a* $(1, 3)$*-ordering problem*

The first step consists of computing the EOQ of each retailer when it acts individually. As there is no fixed purchasing cost, retailers prefer the stand-alone position.

When $\boldsymbol{a} \neq \mathbf{0}$, retailers are tempted to form coalitions in order to share the fixed ordering cost a.

3.4.3. *Quantity-dependent purchasing price*

An alternative policy of the supplier can draw a price landing expressed in terms of the quantity to be ordered. This pricing strategy is expressed in the following way: regarding equation [2.3], the supplier offers the opportunity to benefit from a reduced price if the ordered quantity exceeds a prefixed threshold termed $quantity$.

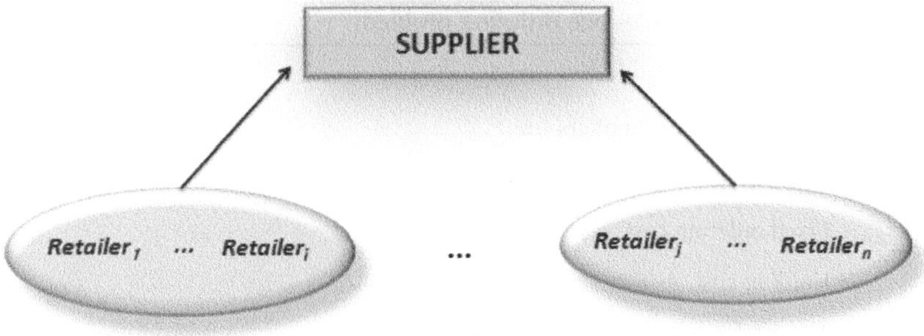

Figure 3.3. *A supply chain with one supplier and multiple retailers*

3.5. The multiple suppliers–one retailer ordering problem

This ordering variant, which involves one retailer that tries to order from one among a set of suppliers, involves two main steps already stated in Table 3.1:

1) *Supplier selection*: the retailer should at first produce a comparative analysis between all suppliers' total costs depending on the quantity to be ordered and prices' landings, if any. This step is alternatively expressed as follows, given the retailer's demand d:

SUPPLIER SELECTION

$$\begin{array}{lll}
\boldsymbol{Supplier_1} & Price_1(d) \xrightarrow{TC\ Computation} & TC_1(d) \\
\boldsymbol{Supplier_2} & Price_2(d) \xrightarrow{TC\ Computation} & TC_2(d) \\
\vdots & & \\
\boldsymbol{Supplier_m} & Price_m(d) \xrightarrow{TC\ Computation} & TC_m(d) \\
\hline
\multicolumn{3}{l}{\boldsymbol{Best\ \ supplier}\ Supplier_j \Rightarrow TC_j(d) = Min_{i=1}^{m} TC_i(d)}
\end{array}$$

2) *EOQ computation*: once the appropriate supplier is selected, the whole quantity to be ordered d should be divided into equal portions gradually along the time period. Below are the two equations related to the EOQ computation:

Demand per period	*Number of periods*
$q^* = \sqrt{\frac{2da}{h}}$	$m^* = \frac{d}{q^*}$

Algorithm 2: The multiple–one ordering problem

1. Input data

- Total number of suppliers: m
- Purchasing costs: $p_1, \ldots, p_m$
- Fixed ordering cost: a
- Holding cost: h
- The total quantity to be ordered: d

2. Ordering process

1) Select the most cost saving supplier

2) Compute the EOQ

3. Output data

- j: the selected supplier
- q^*: the optimal quantity to be ordered at each period
- m^*: the optimal number of orders

3.6. The multiple suppliers–multiple retailers ordering problem

A more generalized version of the ordering activity is to extend the two problem dimensions to multiple suppliers and multiple retailers. This enlargement of the problem modeling involves, as mentioned in Table 3.1, the following tasks:

– *Stand-alone scenario*:

- individual EOQ computing;
- supplier selection.

– *Coalitional scenario*:

- collaboration;
- collaborative EOQ computing.

In the following, we detail the main guidelines of each scenario. Then, both scenarios are to be compared to adopt the most cost saving one.

1) *Stand-alone scenario*

Following is the modeling design of the stand-alone operation.

– *Individual EOQ computing*: For each firm *i*, the EOQ q_i^* *i* related to its individual demand d_i is computed, giving rise to the optimal number of periods m_i^*, using the following equations:

Optimal quantity	**Number of periods**
$q_i^* = \sqrt{\frac{2d_i a_i}{h_i}}$	$m_i^* = \frac{d_i}{q_i^*}$

The following vector is an output for the supplier selection related to each firm:

$$Individual_{EOQ} = [\underbrace{(q_1^*, m_1^*)}_{Firm_1}, \underbrace{(q_2^*, m_2^*)}_{Firm_2}, \ldots, \underbrace{(q_n^*, m_n^*)}_{Firm_n}] \qquad [3.8]$$

– *Supplier selection*: Each firm is asked to select, from a set of suppliers, the appropriate one depending on:

- the ordering price offered by each supplier j ($j = 1, \ldots, m$);
- the quantity to be ordered by firm i ($i = 1, \ldots, n$).

Based on these two components, the ordering problem can be viewed as the optimization of ordering cost of each firm i while fulfilling some structural constraints. Hence, each firm i should minimize its total cost split into the effective ordering cost and the supplier selection cost.

Given the following problem data, we can clearly model the $m - n$ supplier selection problem as follows:

Inputs	*Outputs*
n: number of firms m: number of suppliers q_i^*: the quantity to be ordered per period of firm i m_i^*: the number of periods for firm i c_p^j: the unit ordering price of supplier j d_i: the demand of firm i	$y_j = \begin{cases} 1 & \text{if supplier } j \text{is selected} \\ 0 & \text{otherwise} \end{cases}$

Table 3.4. *Inputs/outputs of the $m - n$ ordering problem*

FOR EACH FIRM $i = 1, \ldots, n$

OBJECTIVE *Minimize the total cost of firm i*
S. t.
CONSTRAINTS
– *The total quantity to be ordered* $\leq$ *the demand of firm i*
– *Firm i should select only one supplier*

The above specification is mathematically expressed as follows:

$$\begin{aligned} & Min\ z(x) = \sum_{j=1}^{m} \sum_{t=1}^{T} p_j q_{it} y_j + \sum_{j=1}^{m} s_j y_j \\ & S.t. \\ & \quad \sum_{t=1}^{m_i^*} q_i^* y_j \leq d_i \\ & \quad \sum_{j=1}^{m} y_j = 1 \\ & \quad y_j \in \{0,1\} \end{aligned} \qquad [3.9]$$

2) *Coalitional scenario*

– *Collaboration*: The coalition formation allows the grouping of some orders in a way that allows firms to considerably reduce their ordering costs. In fact, the ordering price is generally inversely proportional to the quantity to be ordered. This task is costly, as the number of possible coalitions is, given n firms:

$2^n - 1$ coalitions

The generated coalition structures are then evaluated according to their total ordering costs:

$$\begin{aligned} & CS^1 = \{Coalition_1, \ldots, Coalition_{k_1}\} \Rightarrow Cost(CS^1) \\ & CS^2 = \{Coalition_1, \ldots, Coalition_{k_2}\} \Rightarrow Cost(CS^2) \\ & \vdots \\ & CS^h = \{Coalition_1, \ldots, Coalition_{k_h}\} \Rightarrow Cost(CS^h) \end{aligned}$$

$$CS^* = \{Coalition_1, \ldots, Coalition_{k^*}\} \Rightarrow Cost(CS^*)$$

where $Cost(CS^*)$ corresponds to the minimum cost, i.e.:

$$Cost(CS^*) = Min_k Cost(CS^k) \qquad [3.10]$$

– *Collaborative EOQ computing:* Once the best coalition structure CS^* is generated, the quantity to be ordered for each coalition is computed. Assuming that all firms have the same fixed ordering cost a and the same unit holding cost h, the EOQ computation that generates, for each firm k:

- Q_k^*: the quantity to be ordered per period;
- M_k^*: the appropriate number of periods;

is expressed in terms of the coalition's demand as follows:

$$Coalition_1\text{: } D_1 = \sum_{f=1}^{nb^1} d_f \Rightarrow Q_1^* = \sqrt{\frac{2D_1 a}{h}} \text{ and } M_1^* = \frac{D_1}{Q_1^*}$$
$$Coalition_2\text{: } D_2 = \sum_{f=1}^{nb^2} d_f \Rightarrow Q_2^* = \sqrt{\frac{2D_2 a}{h}} \text{ and } M_2^* = \frac{D_2}{Q_2^*}$$
$$\vdots$$
$$Coalition_{k^*}\text{: } D_{k^*} = \sum_{f=1}^{nb^{k^*}} d_f \Rightarrow Q_{k^*}^* = \sqrt{\frac{2D_{k^*} a}{h}} \text{ and } M_{k^*}^* = \frac{D_{k^*}}{Q_{k^*}^*}$$

The following vector is an output for the supplier selection related to each coalition:

$$Collaborative_{EOQ} = [\underbrace{(Q_1^*, M_1^*)}_{Coalition_1}, \underbrace{(Q_2^*, M_2^*)}_{Coalition_2}, \ldots, \underbrace{(Q_{k^*}^*, M_{k^*})}_{Coalition_{k^*}}] \qquad [3.11]$$

Algorithm 3: The m - n ordering problem

---

1. Input data

- m: the number of suppliers
- n: the number of firms
- c_j^p: the ordering price of each supplier

2. Ordering process

- *Supplier selection:* Each firm supplier's offer depending on the ordered quantity
- *Stand-alone situation:* Compute for each firm its individual ordering cost
- *Coalitional situation:* Coalition formation of the firms in order to gather their orders for cost saving
- *For each firm:* Compare the coalitional and the stand alone costs

2. Output data

The best configuration: Assign each firm to one supplier and a coalition
Compute the ordering cost for each firm

3.7. Conclusion

The ordering problem, perceived as a key activity in the SC, requires the definition of a series of data inputs to be well studied. The ordering problem consists of specifying the appropriate supplier and the price to be selected in order to save the total ordering cost. In this chapter we analyzed four potential situations characterized by the number of suppliers (one or many) and the number of firms (one or many). In each situation, numerous steps are to be followed, namely the supplier selection and the eventual collaborations that may occur between firms. Once these steps are accomplished, the quantity to be ordered should be dispatched within a time period in order to benefit from delaying ordered quantities. The study of the previously announced ordering problems shows the effectiveness of adopting a collaborative standpoint. Indeed, in a case of multiple suppliers, the supplier selection improves the total ordering cost when compared to a random supplier selection. For a multiple firms ordering problem, the collaboration is expressed in terms of coalitions designed as joint orderings. In such cases, the cost gap of the coalitional and the stand-alone situations is the best incentive for firms to reduce their individual ordering costs.

4

The Warehousing Problem

4.1. Introduction

One of the most discussed problems in the supply chain (SC) is the storage of firms' items aiming at minimizing their costs while trying to fulfill numerous resource constraints. In this chapter, we consider an SC network where firms attempt to design a storage plan, given a prefixed number of facilities, and distribute them to a set of customers. The possible rented facilities are determined through a signal sent by other companies about their remaining capacities as well as their proposed rent costs. The aim is the collaboration of different companies through sharing storage capacities to improve logistics efficiency and cost saving. In the context of supply chain management, collaboration can be applied by sharing transportation capacity (CO3 project), warehousing capacity [CAR 10] as well as resource capacity [BER 11]. The collaboration in transportation is accomplished by shared truckloads that periodically shuttle between companies' customers. The warehousing capacity concerns shared/common warehouses to be used by a set of collaborative companies and the resource capacity consists of sharing customer demands. Considering these three types of capacity sharing can influence the design of the network as costs can be reduced by using a collaborative network. In fact, a set of facilities must be deployed to keep a high service level and at the lowest cost. To do so, each company must analyze the potential and already existing networks according to their customers' needs. Hence, for a given planning horizon, the set of facilities to be used is determined through opening and sharing decisions. Used resources can then be classified into public and private facilities according to the customers' requirements. For this, common storage of items can be a challenging and cost-saving solution. In the following, firms are tempted to form coalitions to share common warehouses. A coalition is defined by the set of companies that accept to share the same warehouses. This study aims to take the initial steps of the way the performance impact on the supply chain design can be increased by using ideas and features of the collaboration in the warehousing. We detail in this chapter four problem variants that differ in terms of the cost structure and the possibility of conflicts that may occur between items. This chapter is structured as follows. Section 4.2 states the Warehousing Problem (WP) followed by its eventual features' extensions and the terminology adopted throughout the WP description. Subsequent sections address the main four WP variants: their specificities and problem descriptions. Illustrative examples follow to show the effectiveness of such optimization modelings.

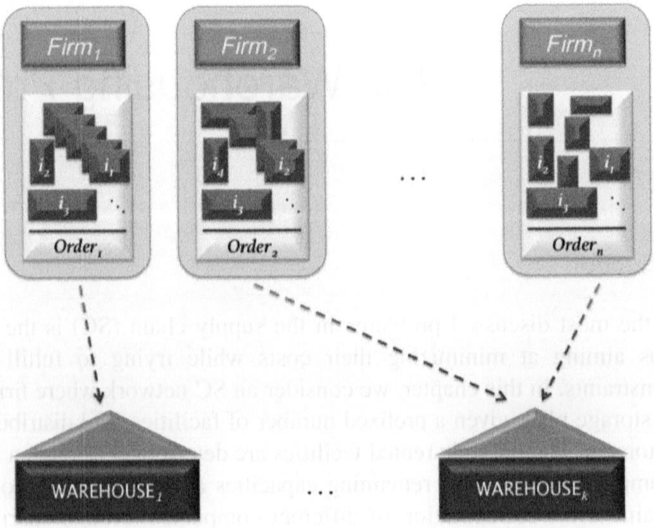

Figure 4.1. *Main steps of the warehousing problem*

4.2. Problem description

Given a set of firms characterized by their orders and a set of warehouses with capacities known in advance, the warehousing problem consists of storing all firms' orders in the warehouses in such a way to minimize the holding cost. Numerous variants of the warehousing problem are of interest depending on the cost to be incurred by the firms, as follows:

– *variable cost warehousing problem:* in which case each order, characterized by its weight, has a cost that depends on the warehouse;

– *fixed cost warehousing problem*: which requires a cost for each hired warehouse.

Moreover, items can be in conflict; therefore, we point out two possible scenarios:

– *non-conflicting items:* there does not exist any conflict between pairs of items;

– *conflicts between items:* some pairs of items should not be stored in the same warehouse. This is due to some feature incompatibilities.

We develop in the remainder of this chapter the main features of each warehousing configuration and model its mathematical model. Then, we detail a relevant problem variant that takes into account the possibility of conflicts between items.

4.2.1. *Terminology*

Below, we list the major symbols used in the mathematical model.

– Parameters

n	Number of orders
k	Number of warehouses
C	Cost matrix
W_j	Warehouse j's capacity
w_i	Weight of order i
$Conflict_{(n\times n)}$	A square binary matrix that displays 1 if orders a and b are in conflict, and 0 otherwise

The cost matrix C depends on the cost protocol, as mentioned in section 4.2. The variable cost requires the input of a unit warehousing cost c_{ij} which depends on order i and warehouse j, expressed in a matrix $C_{(n\times k)}$. However, if the warehousing cost depends only on the warehouse, the cost matrix is designed as a line vector $C_{(1\times k)}$ that provides the cost of renting each warehouse j. We detail hereafter the mathematical expression of the warehousing cost related to each situation.

Variable cost WP	Fixed cost WP
– Cost matrix $C_{(n\times k)} = \begin{pmatrix} c_{11} & c_{12} & \cdots & c_{1k} \\ c_{11} & c_{12} & \cdots & c_{1k} \\ \vdots & \ddots & & \\ c_{n1} & c_{n2} & \cdots & c_{nk} \end{pmatrix}$	- Cost matrix $C_{(1\times k)} = (c_1, c_2, \ \ldots \ , c_k)$
– Objective function $Min\ z(x) = \sum_{i=1}^{n}\sum_{j=1}^{k} c_{ij}x_{ij}$	- Objective function $Min\ z(x) = \sum_{j=1}^{k} c_j y_j$

– Decision variables $y_k = \begin{cases} 1 \text{ if bin } k \text{is used} \\ 0 \text{ otherwise} \end{cases}$ $x_{ik} = \begin{cases} 1 \text{ if item } i \text{ is assigned} \\ 0 \text{ to bin } k \text{ otherwise} \end{cases}$

For all WP configurations, the output is the storage configuration matrix $x_{(n\times m)}$ that expresses the placement x_{ij} of order i in warehouse j expressed as follows:

$$x = \begin{pmatrix} x_{11}\ x_{12}\ \dots\ x_{1m} \\ x_{21}\ x_{22}\ \dots\ x_{2m} \\ \vdots \quad \ddots \end{pmatrix} \qquad [4.1]$$
$$\Downarrow$$
$$\text{if } \sum_{i=1}^{n} x_{ij} \geq 1, j = 1, \dots, m \Rightarrow y_j = 1$$

Equation [4.1] outputs the placement of the whole set of n items in the m warehouses, knowing that the optimization process tries to use the minimum number of warehouses in the sense that the total cost is minimized. In fact, the decision variable is y_j, which indicates whether a warehouse j is used or not. In such a case, if an item is placed in a warehouse, the corresponding warehouse should be labeled as used. This is mathematically expressed by $y_j = 1$.

4.2.2. *Inputs/outputs of the WP*

The inputs and outputs of the WP are reported in the following table.

Inputs	*Outputs*
n: the number of firms	$y_j = \begin{cases} 1 \text{ if warehouse } j \text{is used} \\ 0 \text{ otherwise} \end{cases}$
k: the number of warehouses	
W_j the capacity of warehouse j	w_i: the weight of firm i's order
	$x_{ik} = \begin{cases} 1 \text{ if demand of customer } i \text{is assigned} \\ 0 \text{ to warehouse } k \text{ otherwise} \end{cases}$

4.2.3. *WP variants*

The WP is defined through a set of features that determine a specific class in terms of cost and item compatibilities. Hence, we point out the following possibilities:

– *cost:* variable cost *or* fixed cost;

– *item compatibilities:* without conflict *or* with conflict.

According to Table 4.1, four warehousing configurations are of interest. We detail in what follows the main features of each problem configuration:

– *WP with variable cost/without conflicts:* the WP in its current version requires the minimization of a warehouse-dependent cost function already input as a cost matrix that reports the unit cost given to an item i ($i = 1, \ldots, n$) and a warehouse j ($j = 1, \ldots, k$). Hence, the cost matrix C is sized $(n \times k)$. System constraints include the placement requirements that assign each firm's order in one warehouse. Furthermore, capacity constraints generate feasible solutions in the sense that each warehouse, characterized by its storage capacity, should respect such requirements.

	Variable cost	*Fixed cost*
Without conflict	*Min.* *Var. cost* *S.t.* *- Assignment constr.* *- Capacity constr.*	*Min.* *Fix. cost* *S.t.* *- Assignment constr.* *- Capacity constr.*
With conflict	*Min.* *Var. cost* *S.t.* *- Assignment constr.* *- Capacity constr.* *- Conflicts constr.*	*Min.* *Fix. cost* *S.t.* *- Assignment constr.* *- Capacity constr.* *- Conflicts constr.*

Table 4.1. *Warehousing problem configurations in terms of cost and item conflicts*

– *WP with fixed cost/without conflicts:* the cost function to be minimized can be seen from an alternative point of view that assumes a fixed warehousing cost for each warehouse, once used for the storage activity. Regarding such an assumption, the objective function should be modeled in terms of the used warehouses and the consequent costs.

– *WP with variable cost/with conflicts:* this version of the WP assumes both variability in the cost function, leading to the use of the C matrix, and the possibility of incompatibilities between items. Based on these assumptions, a new series of constraints, that impose the storage of orders, can arise regarding those incompatibilities.

– *WP with fixed cost/with conflicts:* the WP can be seen as the storage of the whole set of items regarding the possible conflicts during the storage process and the consideration, in the computation of the cost function, of a fixed warehousing cost allocated to the use of each warehouse. The mathematical model, described in the remainder of this chapter, should take into account such considerations.

We proceed in what follows with a detailed description of the four WP variants.

4.3. WP with variable cost/without conflicts

4.3.1. *Mathematical formulation*

Mathematical model [4.6] corresponds to the variable cost warehousing problem assuming that no conflict exists between orders:

$$\begin{array}{ll} Min\ z(x) = \sum_{i=1}^{n} \sum_{j=1}^{k} c_{ij}x_{ij} & \\ S.t. & \\ \quad \sum_{i=1}^{n} w_j x_{ij} \leq W_j y_j & j = 1, \ldots, k \\ \quad \sum_{j=1}^{k} x_{ij} = 1 & i = 1, \ldots, n \end{array} \qquad [4.2]$$

Mathematical formulation [4.6] refers to the optimization of the warehousing cost while fulfilling structural constraint as detailed hereafter:

– Objective function: *minimize the warehouse and order-dependent warehousing cost.*

– Constraints:

- capacity requirements;

- placement constraints.

4.3.2. *An example*

Let us consider a warehousing problem that handles a set of $n = 6$ orders to be stored in $k = 4$ warehouses. It is assumed that storage costs of orders depend on the selected warehouse. Therefore, the cost matrix C reporting the unit cost related to order i and warehousing j is sized (6×4):

$$C = \begin{pmatrix} 2 & 3 & 5 & 8 \\ 10 & 4 & 9 & 11 \\ 5 & 1 & 17 & 20 \\ 11 & 9 & 40 & 25 \\ 4 & 16 & 8 & 45 \\ 60 & 20 & 13 & 25 \end{pmatrix}$$

Hence, the inputs/outputs of the WP are stated as follows:

Inputs	*Outputs*
$n = 6$	$y_{j\,(j=1,\ldots,4)} = \begin{cases} 1 & \text{if warehouse } j \text{ is used} \\ 0 & \text{otherwise} \end{cases}$
$k = 4$	
$(w_1, w_2, w_3, w_4, w_5, w_6) = (50, 80, 35, 60, 50, 45)$	$x_{ik\,(i=1\ldots,6,j=1,\ldots 4)} = \begin{cases} 1 & \text{if order of firm } i \\ & \text{is assigned to} \\ 0 & \text{warehouse } k \text{ otherwise} \end{cases}$
$(W_1, W_2, W_3, W_4) = (100, 150, 120, 200)$	

$$\begin{array}{ll} Min & z(x) = \sum_{i=1}^{6} \sum_{j=1}^{4} c_{ij} x_{ij} \\ S.t. & \\ & \sum_{i=1}^{6} w_j x_{ij} \leq W_j y_j, j = 1, \ldots, 4 \\ & \sum_{j=1}^{4} x_{ij} = 1, i = 1, \ldots, 6 \end{array} \Rightarrow$$

$$\begin{array}{ll} Min & z(x) = 2x_{11} + 3x_{12} + 5x_{13} + 8x_{14} + 10x_{21} + \\ & 4x_{22} + 9x_{23} + x_{24}11 + 5x_{31} + x_{32} + 17x_{33} + \\ & 20x_{34} + 11x_{41} + 9x_{42} + 40x_{43} + 25x_{41} + \\ & 4x_{51} + 16x_{52} + 8x_{53} + 45x_{54} + 60x_{61} + \\ & 20x_{62} + 13x_{63} + 25x_{64} \\ S.t. & \\ & 50x_{11} + 80x_{21} + 35x_{31} + 60x_{41} + 50x_{51} + \\ & 45x_{61} \leq 100 \\ & 50x_{12} + 80x_{22} + 35x_{32} + 60x_{42} + 50x_{52} + \\ & 45x_{62} \leq 150 \\ & 50x_{13} + 80x_{23} + 35x_{33} + 60x_{43} + 50x_{53} + \\ & 45x_{63} \leq 120 \\ & 50x_{14} + 80x_{24} + 35x_{34} + 60x_{44} + 50x_{54} + \\ & 45x_{64} \leq 200 \\ & \\ & x_{11} + x_{12} + x_{13} + x_{14} = 1 \\ & x_{21} + x_{22} + x_{23} + x_{24} = 1 \\ & x_{31} + x_{32} + x_{33} + x_{34} = 1 \\ & x_{41} + x_{42} + x_{43} + x_{44} = 1 \\ & x_{51} + x_{52} + x_{53} + x_{54} = 1 \\ & x_{61} + x_{62} + x_{63} + x_{64} = 1 \end{array}$$

The optimizer outputs the following optimal solution x^*:

Output of the Optimizer	*Solution details* $z(x^*) = 23$
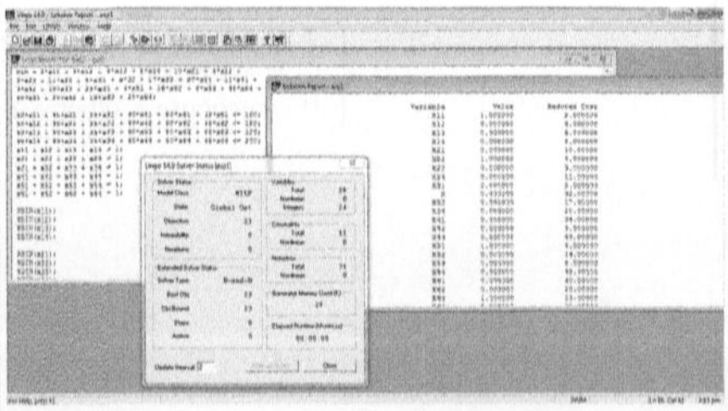	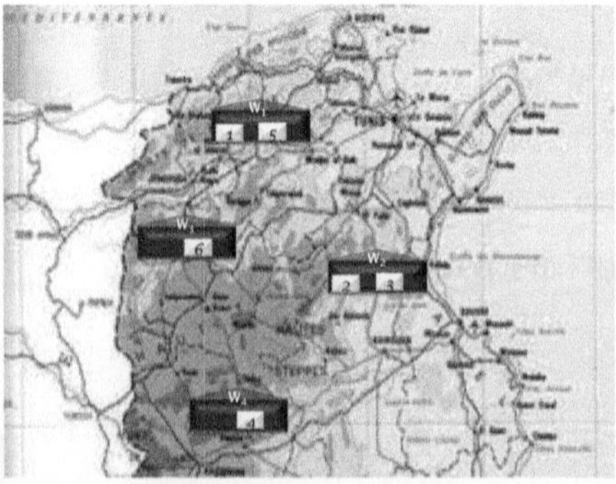

4.4. WP with fixed cost/without conflicts

In this case, each warehouse is characterized by its cost. Once a firm i decides to store its goods in warehouse *j*, it should incur the whole warehousing cost whatever the quantity might be. The incentive behind a cooperation in the warehousing is the share of this warehousing cost that does not depend on the stored quantity.

4.4.1. *Mathematical formulation*

The mathematical model related to the fixed cost warehousing problem is expressed in optimization problem [4.3]:

$$
\begin{array}{ll}
Min\ z(x) = \sum_{j=1}^{k} c_j y_j & \\
S.t. & \\
\quad \sum_{i=1}^{n} w_j x_{ij} \leq W_j y_j & j = 1, \ldots, k \\
\quad \sum_{j=1}^{k} x_{ij} = 1 & i = 1, \ldots, n
\end{array}
\qquad [4.3]
$$

4.4.2. *An example*

Let us consider a warehousing problem that handles $n = 6$ firms and $k = 4$ warehouses, as stated in the previous example. We assume that fixed costs are assigned to warehouses.

Hence, the inputs/outputs of the WP are stated as follows:

Inputs	*Outputs*
$n = 6$	$y_{j\,(j=1,\ldots,4)} = \begin{cases} 1 & \text{if warehouse } j \text{ is used} \\ 0 & \text{otherwise} \end{cases}$
$k = 4$	
$C_{(1,\ldots,4)} = (700, 1000, 1500, 800)$	
$(w_1, w_2, w_3, w_4, w_5, w_6) =$	$x_{ik\,(i=1\ldots,6,j=1,\ldots 4)} = \begin{cases} 1 & \text{if order of firm } i \\ & \text{is assigned to warehouse } k \\ 0 & \text{otherwise} \end{cases}$
$(50, 80, 35, 60, 50, 45)$	
$(W_1, W_2, W_3, W_4) = (100, 150, 120, 200)$	

$$
\begin{array}{ll}
Min & z(x) = \sum_{j=1}^{4} c_j y_j \\
S.t. & \\
& \sum_{i=1}^{6} w_j x_{ij} \leq W_j y_j, j = 1, \ldots, 4 \\
& \sum_{j=1}^{4} x_{ij} = 1, i = 1, \ldots, 6
\end{array}
\Rightarrow
$$

$$
\begin{array}{ll}
Min & z(x) = 700y_1 + 1000y_2 + 1500y_3 + 800y_4 \\
S.t. & \\
& 50x_{11} + 80x_{21} + 35x_{31} + 60x_{41} + 50x_{51} + \\
& 45x_{61} \leq 100y_1 \\
& 50x_{12} + 80x_{22} + 35x_{32} + 60x_{42} + 50x_{52} + \\
& 45x_{62} \leq 150y_2 \\
& 50x_{13} + 80x_{23} + 35x_{33} + 60x_{43} + 50x_{53} + \\
& 45x_{63} \leq 120y_3 \\
& 50x_{14} + 80x_{24} + 35x_{34} + 60x_{44} + 50x_{54} + \\
& 45x_{64} \leq 200y_4 \\
& x_{11} + x_{12} + x_{13} + x_{14} = 1 \\
& x_{21} + x_{22} + x_{23} + x_{24} = 1 \\
& x_{31} + x_{32} + x_{33} + x_{34} = 1 \\
& x_{41} + x_{42} + x_{43} + x_{44} = 1 \\
& x_{51} + x_{52} + x_{53} + x_{54} = 1 \\
& x_{61} + x_{62} + x_{63} + x_{64} = 1
\end{array}
$$

The optimal solution's details, as output by the optimizer, are the following:

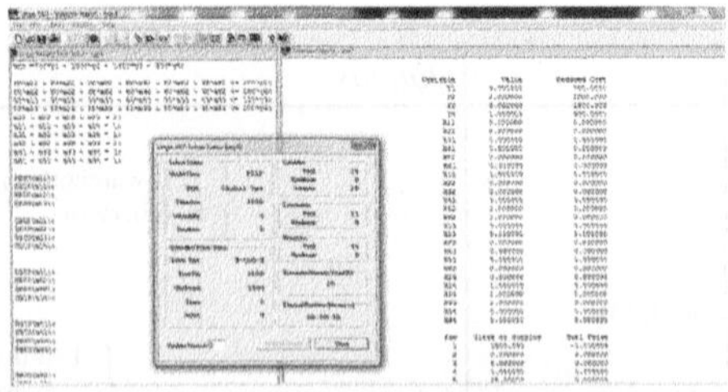

$$\Downarrow$$

$$\boxed{z(x^*) = 1800}$$

$$(y_1, y_2, y_3, y_4) = (0, 1, 0, 1) \Rightarrow \textit{2 warehouses are used}$$

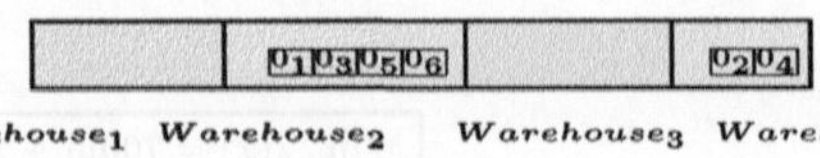

4.5. WP with variable cost/with conflicts

In many situations, partners in the SC are tempted to minimize their storage costs while taking into account conflicts between pairs of items in the warehousing process. A predefined number of items, with different weights, are to be stored in a set of warehouses with fixed capacities. The objective of the firms involved is to minimize the number of bins used while respecting the incompatibility constraints in the storage of some pairs of items. This problem is appropriately modeled as shown in Table 4.1. In fact, some of the considered items' categories are incompatible and cannot be jointly stored in the same warehouse. We model these conflicts in the following the fact that if two orders are in conflict, at most one of the corresponding placement decision variables should take 1. This requirement is modeled as follows:

$$\text{if orders } a \text{ and } b \text{ are in conflict} \Rightarrow x_{aj} + x_{bj} \leq 1, \;\; j = 1, \ldots, k \qquad [4.4]$$

These conflicts are summarized in the binary square matrix $Conflict_{(n \times n)}$ that displays 1 if orders a and b are in conflict and 0 otherwise. Thus, we symbolize:

– $Conflict(a, b) = 1$ if orders a and b are in conflict.

– $Conflict(a, b) = 0$ otherwise.

4.5.1. *Mathematical formulation*

Let us consider hereafter an alternative WP formulation that assumes variable costs and the possibility of order incompatibilities between pairs of orders.

$$
\begin{array}{lr}
Min\ z(x) = \sum_{i=1}^{n} \sum_{j=1}^{k} c_{ij} x_{ij} & \\
S.t. & \\
\quad \sum_{i=1}^{n} w_j x_{ij} \leq W_j y_j \qquad j = 1, \ldots, k & \\
\quad x_{aj} + x_{bj} \leq 1, \ \ j = 1, \ldots, k, Conflict(a, b) = 1 & \\
\quad \sum_{j=1}^{k} x_{ij} = 1 \qquad i = 1, \ldots, n &
\end{array}
\qquad [4.5]
$$

Mathematical formulation [4.6] refers to the optimization of the warehousing cost while fulfilling structural constraints as detailed hereafter:

– Objective function: *minimize the warehouse and order-dependent warehousing cost.*

– Constraints:

- capacity requirements;

- conflicting order constraints;

- placement constraints.

4.5.2. *An example*

Let us consider a warehousing problem that handles a set of $n = 6$ orders to be stored in $k = 4$ warehouses. It is assumed that orders' storage costs depend on the selected warehouse. Therefore, the cost matrix C reporting the unit cost related to order i and warehousing j is sized (6×4):

$$
C = \begin{pmatrix} 2 & 3 & 5 & 8 \\ 10 & 4 & 9 & 11 \\ 5 & 1 & 17 & 20 \\ 11 & 9 & 40 & 25 \\ 4 & 16 & 8 & 45 \\ 60 & 20 & 13 & 25 \end{pmatrix}
$$

Hence, the inputs/outputs of the WP are stated as follows:

Inputs	*Outputs*
$n = 6$	$y_{j\,(j=1,\ldots,4)} = \begin{cases} 1 & \text{if warehouse } j \text{ is used} \\ 0 & \text{otherwise} \end{cases}$
$k = 4$	
$(w_1, w_2, w_3, w_4, w_5, w_6) =$ $(50, 80, 35, 60, 50, 45)$	$x_{ik\,(i=1\ldots,6,\ j=1,\ldots 4)} = \begin{cases} 1 & \text{if order of firm } i \text{ is assigned to warehouse } j \\ 0 & \text{otherwise} \end{cases}$
$(W_1, W_2, W_3, W_4) = (100, 150, 120, 200)$	
$Conflicts_{(6\times 6)} = \begin{pmatrix} 0&0&0&1&0&0 \\ 0&0&1&0&0&0 \\ 0&1&0&0&1&0 \\ 1&0&0&0&0&0 \\ 0&0&1&0&0&0 \\ 0&0&0&0&0&0 \end{pmatrix}$	

The conflict matrix presented in the above inputs/outputs gives rise to three conflicting pairs of orders, numbered from 1 to 3, as follows:

1	2	3
$\underbrace{\{1,4\}}$	$\underbrace{\{2,3\}}$	$\underbrace{\{3,5\}}$
1 and 4 in conflict	*2 and 3 in conflict*	*3 and 5 in conflict*

Hence, three sets of constraints should be inserted in the mathematical model. Each set of constraints corresponding to the pair $\{a, b\}$ forbids the joint storage of orders a and b in the same warehouse, therefore the mathematical formulation of the WP with variable cost and taking into account three pairwise conflicts is written in the following way:

$$
\begin{array}{lll}
Min & z(x) = \sum_{i=1}^{6} \sum_{j=1}^{4} c_{ij} x_{ij} & \\
S.t. & & \\
& \sum_{i=1}^{6} w_j x_{ij} \leq W_j y_j & j = 1, \ldots, 4 \\
& x_{1j} + x_{4j} \leq 1 & j = 1, \ldots, 4 \\
& x_{2j} + x_{3j} \leq 1 & j = 1, \ldots, 4 \\
& x_{3j} + x_{5j} \leq 1 & j = 1, \ldots, 4 \\
& \sum_{j=1}^{4} x_{ij} = 1 & i = 1, \ldots, 6
\end{array}
$$

$\Downarrow$

$$\begin{aligned}
\textbf{\textit{Min}}\quad & z(x) = 2x_{11} + 3x_{12} + 5x_{13} + 8x_{14} + 10x_{21} + 4x_{22} + 9x_{23} + x_{24}11 + 5x_{31} + x_{32} + \\
& 17x_{33} + 20x_{34} + 11x_{41} + 9x_{42} + 40x_{43} + 25x_{41} + 4x_{51} + 16x_{52} + 8x_{53} + 45x_{54} + \\
& 60x_{61} + 20x_{62} + 13x_{63} + 25x_{64}
\end{aligned}$$

$S.t.$

– *Capacity requirements*
$$\begin{cases} 50x_{11} + 80x_{21} + 35x_{31} + 60x_{41} + 50x_{51} + 45x_{61} \leq 100 \\ 50x_{12} + 80x_{22} + 35x_{32} + 60x_{42} + 50x_{52} + 45x_{62} \leq 150 \\ 50x_{13} + 80x_{23} + 35x_{33} + 60x_{43} + 50x_{53} + 45x_{63} \leq 120 \\ 50x_{14} + 80x_{24} + 35x_{34} + 60x_{44} + 50x_{54} + 45x_{64} \leq 200 \end{cases}$$

– *Conflicts of 1 and 4*
$$\begin{cases} x_{11} + x_{41} \leq 1 \\ x_{12} + x_{42} \leq 1 \\ x_{13} + x_{43} \leq 1 \\ x_{14} + x_{44} \leq 1 \end{cases}$$

– *Conflicts of 2 and 3*
$$\begin{cases} x_{21} + x_{31} \leq 1 \\ x_{22} + x_{32} \leq 1 \\ x_{23} + x_{33} \leq 1 \\ x_{24} + x_{34} \leq 1 \end{cases}$$

– *Conflicts of 3 and 5*
$$\begin{cases} x_{31} + x_{51} \leq 1 \\ x_{32} + x_{52} \leq 1 \\ x_{33} + x_{53} \leq 1 \\ x_{34} + x_{54} \leq 1 \end{cases}$$

– *Placement constraints*
$$\begin{cases} x_{11} + x_{12} + x_{13} + x_{14} = 1 \\ x_{21} + x_{22} + x_{23} + x_{24} = 1 \\ x_{31} + x_{32} + x_{33} + x_{34} = 1 \\ x_{41} + x_{42} + x_{43} + x_{44} = 1 \\ x_{51} + x_{52} + x_{53} + x_{54} = 1 \\ x_{61} + x_{62} + x_{63} + x_{64} = 1 \end{cases}$$

The optimizer outputs the following optimal solution x^*:

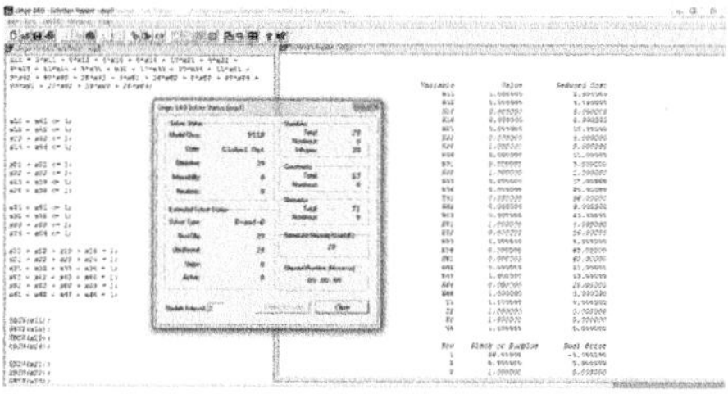

$$\Downarrow$$

$$\boxed{z(x^*) = 29}$$

$$(y_1, y_2, y_3, y_4) = (1, 1, 1, 1) \Rightarrow \textit{4 warehouses are used}$$

$O_1 O_5$	O_3	$O_2 O_6$	$O_1 4$
$\textbf{\textit{Warehouse}}_1$	$\textbf{\textit{Warehouse}}_2$	$\textbf{\textit{Warehouse}}_3$	$\textbf{\textit{Warehouse}}_4$

4.6. WP with fixed cost/with conflicts

We develop in what follows the fourth WP variant that assumes fixed costs for the rental of warehouses [BEN 15].

4.6.1. *Mathematical formulation*

The WP with $n = 6$ items and $k = 4$ is reconsidered with the objective to minimize a total cost expressed in terms of fixed warehousing cost that depends only on the cost of renting warehouses. Moreover, conflicts between 3 pairs of orders are assumed. The following mathematical model addresses such a WP variant:

$$\begin{array}{ll}
Min\ z(x) = \sum_{i=1}^{n} \sum_{j=1}^{k} c_j y_j & \\
S.t. & \\
\quad \sum_{i=1}^{n} w_j x_{ij} \leq W_j y_j & j = 1, \ldots, k \\
\quad x_{aj} + x_{bj} \leq 1,\ j = 1, \ldots, k, Conflict(a, b) = 1 & \\
\quad \sum_{j=1}^{k} x_{ij} = 1 & i = 1, \ldots, n
\end{array} \qquad [4.6]$$

Mathematical formulation [4.6] refers to the optimization of the warehousing cost while fulfilling structural constraints as detailed hereafter:

– Objective function: *minimize the warehouse-dependent cost.*

– Constraints:

- capacity requirements;
- conflicting order constraints;
- placement constraints.

4.6.2. *An example*

We reconsider again the WP that handles a set of $n = 6$ orders to be stored in $k = 4$ warehouses. It is assumed that orders' storage costs depend on the selected warehouse. Therefore, the cost matrix C reporting the cost related to warehouse j is sized (1×4):

$$C = \begin{pmatrix} 2 & 3 & 5 & 8 \\ 10 & 4 & 9 & 11 \\ 5 & 1 & 17 & 20 \\ 11 & 9 & 40 & 25 \\ 4 & 16 & 8 & 45 \\ 60 & 20 & 13 & 25 \end{pmatrix}$$

Hence, the inputs/outputs of the WP are stated as follows:

Inputs		*Outputs*
$n = 6$		$y_{j\,(j=1,\ldots,4)} = \begin{cases} 1 & \text{if warehouse } j \text{ is used} \\ 0 & \text{otherwise} \end{cases}$
$k = 4$		
$C_{(1,\ldots,4)} = (700, 1000, 1500, 800)$		
$(w_1, w_2, w_3, w_4, w_5, w_6)$	=	$x_{ik\,(i=1\ldots,6,\ j=1,\ldots 4)} = \begin{cases} 1 & \text{if order of firm } i \\ & \text{is assigned to warehouse } j \\ 0 & \text{otherwise} \end{cases}$
$(50, 80, 35, 60, 50, 45)$		
$(W_1, W_2, W_3, W_4) = (100, 150, 120, 200)$		
$Conflicts_{(6\times 6)}$		

As in the previous example, the conflict matrix presented in the above inputs/outputs gives rise to three conflicting pairs of orders, numbered from 1 to 3, as follows:

$$Conflicts_{(6\times 6)}$$

$$\begin{pmatrix} 0&0&0&1&0&0 \\ 0&0&1&0&0&0 \\ 0&1&0&0&1&0 \\ 1&0&0&0&0&0 \\ 0&0&1&0&0&0 \\ 0&0&0&0&0&0 \end{pmatrix}$$

$$\Downarrow$$

Number	1	2	3
Pair	$\{1,4\}$	$\{2,3\}$	$\{3,5\}$

Hence, the following mathematical formulation accounts for the WP with fixed cost and conflicts between three pairs of orders:

$$\begin{array}{lll}
Min & z(x) = \sum_{i=1}^{6} \sum_{j=1}^{4} c_j y_j & \\
S.t. & & \\
& \sum_{i=1}^{6} w_j x_{ij} \leq W_j y_j & j = 1, \ldots, 4 \\
& x_{1j} + x_{4j} \leq 1 & j = 1, \ldots, 4 \\
& x_{2j} + x_{3j} \leq 1 & j = 1, \ldots, 4 \\
& x_{3j} + x_{5j} \leq 1 & j = 1, \ldots, 4 \\
& \sum_{j=1}^{4} x_{ij} = 1 & i = 1, \ldots, 6
\end{array}$$

$$\Downarrow$$

$$\textbf{Min} \quad z(x) = 700y_1 + 1000y_2 + 1500y_3 + 800y_4$$

S.t.

$$\text{– Capacity requirements} \begin{cases} 50x_{11} + 80x_{21} + 35x_{31} + 60x_{41} + 50x_{51} + 45x_{61} \leq 100y_1 \\ 50x_{12} + 80x_{22} + 35x_{32} + 60x_{42} + 50x_{52} + 45x_{62} \leq 150y_2 \\ 50x_{13} + 80x_{23} + 35x_{33} + 60x_{43} + 50x_{53} + 45x_{63} \leq 120y_3 \\ 50x_{14} + 80x_{24} + 35x_{34} + 60x_{44} + 50x_{54} + 45x_{64} \leq 200y_4 \end{cases}$$

$$\text{– Conflicts of 1 and 4} \begin{cases} x_{11} + x_{41} \leq 1 \\ x_{12} + x_{42} \leq 1 \\ x_{13} + x_{43} \leq 1 \\ x_{14} + x_{44} \leq 1 \end{cases}$$

$$\text{– Conflicts of 2 and 3} \begin{cases} x_{21} + x_{31} \leq 1 \\ x_{22} + x_{32} \leq 1 \\ x_{23} + x_{33} \leq 1 \\ x_{24} + x_{34} \leq 1 \end{cases}$$

$$\text{– Conflicts of 3 and 5} \begin{cases} x_{31} + x_{51} \leq 1 \\ x_{32} + x_{52} \leq 1 \\ x_{33} + x_{53} \leq 1 \\ x_{34} + x_{54} \leq 1 \end{cases}$$

$$\text{– Placement constraints} \begin{cases} x_{11} + x_{12} + x_{13} + x_{14} = 1 \\ x_{21} + x_{22} + x_{23} + x_{24} = 1 \\ x_{31} + x_{32} + x_{33} + x_{34} = 1 \\ x_{41} + x_{42} + x_{43} + x_{44} = 1 \\ x_{51} + x_{52} + x_{53} + x_{54} = 1 \\ x_{61} + x_{62} + x_{63} + x_{64} = 1 \end{cases}$$

The optimal solution's details, as output by the optimizer, are the following:

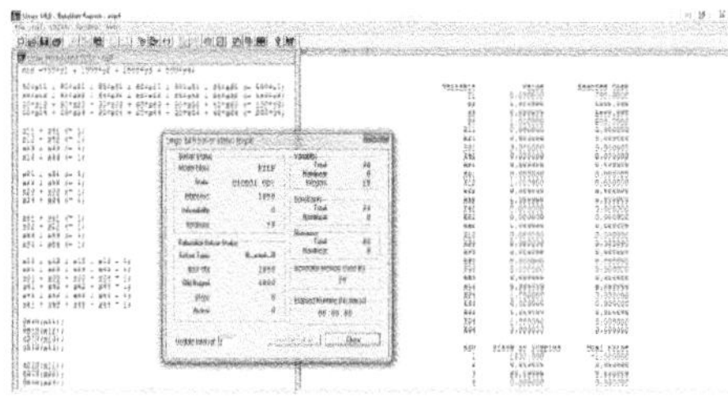

$$\Downarrow$$

$$\boxed{z(x^*) = \mathbf{1800}}$$

$$(y_1, y_2, y_3, y_4) = (0, 1, 0, 1) \Rightarrow \textit{2 warehouses are used}$$

$Warehouse_1$	$Warehouse_2$	$Warehouse_3$	$Warehouse_4$
	O_1 O_3 O_6		O_2 O_4 O_5

4.7. A DSS design for the warehousing problem

As the optimization of the warehousing cost is a relevant component for the SC sustainability, we opt for a Decision Support System (DSS) to solve the storage problems with different sizes. In fact, the implementation of optimization tools inside storage problems is costly due to the complex structure of the optimizers involved and their needs in terms of implementation requirements.

The DSS starts by the extraction of the storage data from the supply chain databases. Figure 4.2 shows the screenshots of the DSS that correspond to the data entry including the number of items, the conflicting items and the bins' features. Such storage data and packing information constitute the inputs for the resolution step. Optimization tools used in the resolution step can either be accomplished by CPLEX or Iterated Local Search (ILS), depending on the problem size, as reported in Figure 4.2. A thorough investigation of the generated solutions in terms of the number of iterations and the processing time illustrates how well the optimization part operates. The DSS outputs the solution to be visualized later in a graphical format.

Regarding Figure 4.2, three screenshots are reported:

a) data inputs are entered in the platform in order to define items' features as costs and weights, and warehouse capacities;

b) the solution approach is selected to be either a cplex optimizer or a benchmark instance from a list of warehousing problems;

c) other parameters are adjusted in the third screenshot as the algorithm that determines the initial solution and the stopping criterion (number of iterations or time).

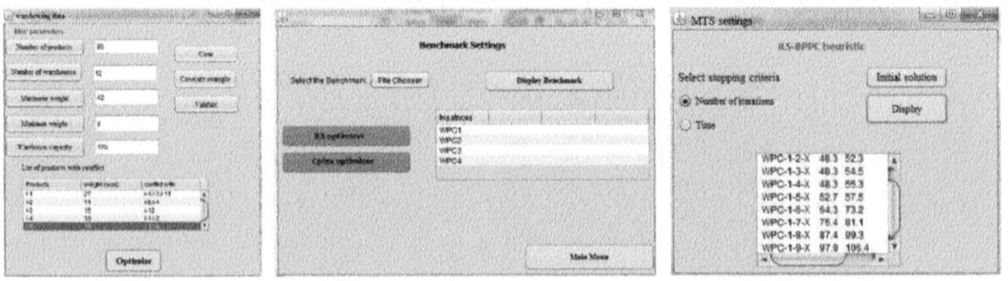

a) b) c)

Figure 4.2. *DSS warehousing interfaces*

4.8. Example

1) Let us consider an ordering problem that involves one supplier and one retailer aiming at ordering 10000 items from a product x with a fixed unit purchasing price of 1^{DT}. The unit holding cost is 5^{DT} and $n = 3$ retailers.

The input data are reported as follows:

Inputs
Retailer 1's demand $d_1 = 5000$
Retailer 2's demand $d_2 = 3000$
Retailer 3's demand $d_3 = 8000$
Purchasing price (per order) $a = 30$
Hoding price $h = 10$
Unit price (from the supplier) $p_1 = 20$

1) Compute the stand-alone position.

2) Compare the following two coalition structures:

$$CS_1 = \{\{1, 2\}, \{3\}\} \text{ and } CS_2 = \{\{1\}, \{2, 3\}\}$$

3) Propose the most cost-saving coalitional form. Explain in detail.

4) What is the gap between the stand-alone situation and the best configuration?

5) Assume that $a = 0$, what is the best configuration?

6) If another supplier is involved in the ordering process where its purchasing price is $p_2 = \begin{cases} 25 \text{ if } q_i \leq 10000 \\ 15 \text{ Otherwise} \end{cases}$ what becomes the best configuration?

4.9. Answer

1) We start by computing the Economic Ordered Quantity (EOQ) for each retailer i $(i = 1, 2, 3)$ expressed in terms of the following mathematical functions: EOQ_i:

$$q_i^* = \sqrt{\frac{2d_i a}{h_i}} \qquad [4.7]$$

Consequently, the optimal number of periods is:

$$m_i^* = \frac{d_i}{q_i^*} \qquad [4.8]$$

The total cost for each retailer is:

$$TC_i = p_1 d_i + a\frac{d_i}{q_i^*} + h\frac{q_i^*}{2} \qquad [4.9]$$

Based on equations [5.4], [4.8] and [5.2], we obtain the optimal ordering values reported and the total cost, reported in Table 3.4.

	q_i^*	m_i^*	TC_i
$Retailer_1$	173.2	29	101 736
$Retailer_2$	134.16	23	61 360.8
$Retailer_3$	219.08	37	162 205.4

Table 4.2. *Economic-order quantities and total costs for the stand-alone position*

2) The total cost for each coalition structure is:

$CS_1 = \{\{1, 2\}, \{3\}\}$:

– EOQ: Let D_1 and $D = 2$ be the demands of the first coalition $A = \{1, 2\}$ and $B = \{3\}$, respectively.

$$D_1 = d_1 + d_2 = 5000 + 3000 = 8000 \text{ and } D_2 = d_3 = 8000$$

Hence, the optimal quantities and frequencies are:

- $Q_1^* = \sqrt{\frac{2\times8000\times30}{10}} = \sqrt{48000} = 219.08$ and $m^* = 37$

- $Q_2^* = \sqrt{\frac{2\times8000\times30}{10}} = \sqrt{48000} = 219.08$ and $m^=37$

For coalition A, the total cost $TC_A = 20\times8000+30\times37+h\frac{219.08}{2} = 162\ 205.4$. For coalition B, the total cost $TC_B = 20 \times 8000 + 30 \times 37 + h\frac{219.08}{2} = 162\ 205.4$.

Let us now compute the individual costs of the retailers regarding the coalition structure CS_1: $TC_1 = TC_A \times \frac{5000}{8000} = 162\ 205.4 \times \frac{5}{8} = 101\ 378.375$ $TC_2 = TC_A \times \frac{3000}{8000} = 162\ 205.4 \times \frac{5}{8} = 38\ 016.890625$ $TC_3 = TC_B = 162\ 205.4$

3) $CS_2 = \{\{1\}, \{2, 3\}\}$:

4.10. Conclusion

The warehousing problem is a significant activity that fully participates in the SC performance in terms of cost and customer satisfaction. The warehousing activity that starts from specifying the set of firms interested in storing orders in warehouses is characterized by the well description of orders' weights and warehouses' capacities. An additional feature that can be relevant in the definition of the warehousing is the possibility of incompatibilities that may occur between orders. Hence, regarding the announced features, four problem configurations were pointed out and illustrated by didactic examples. Such illustrations show how well the warehousing activity can be an incentive for firms to collaborate.

5

Inventory Management

5.1. Introduction

One of the challenging problems in the SC is inventory management, which requires data from the three main entities of the SC, namely suppliers, retailers and customers. It starts from a deep study of customers' demands in order to expect the appropriate ordered quantities while taking into account the quantities in stock. Hence, we can sum up the inventory management to be a master problem that can be handled in terms of the ordering, the warehousing and the delivery costs. In fact, the inventory problem within the SC plays a critical role because it strongly affects the supply chain performances. [LEE 92] considered the inventory control as the only tool to protect supply chain stability, robustness and efficiency in the sense that the computation of all ordered element is online with the stored quantities, customers' demands and the delivery cost. Regarding all such components, the inventory problem positively affects the supply chain sustainability. Based on such concepts, the objective of supply chain inventory management is to satisfy the ultimate customer's demand while increasing the quality and service level and decreasing the total costs. The inventory management system at each supply chain entity (e.g supplier, firm and customer) has to respond to three different questions:

– how often to review the stock status;

– when to order new stock;

– how much stock to be ordered.

The remainder of this chapter is organized as follows. In section 5.2, we define inventory management. Section 5.3 outlines the main purposes of inventory management. Section 5.4 presents the modeling of inventory management.

5.2. Definition of inventory management

Inventory management is defined as a system that supervises the flow of inventories from the suppliers to the customers through a set of intermediate warehouses. As shown by Figure 5.1, inventory management is the control of the stock level through ordering and storage policies that depend on the customers' demands and the suppliers' produce. Alternatively, it keeps a detailed record of each new or returned inventory in the warehouses. Four types of inventory exist:

– *raw material* inventories used to separate suppliers from the production process;

– *work-in-process* used to separate stages of the production process;

– *operating inventories* used to satisfy the needs and the timing of some maintenances and equipment;

– *finished goods* because customer demands may be unknown or the production process cannot respond as rapidly as desired by the customer.

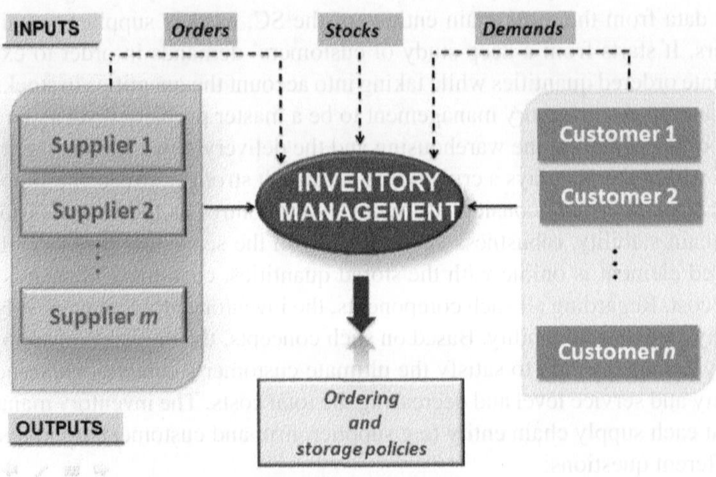

Figure 5.1. *The inventory system*

Following the latter type of inventory, the main objective of the inventory management is to handle the inventories' stock regarding the supplier availability in order to satisfy the customers' needs with suitable delays and to save all of the accompanying costs.

5.3. Purposes of inventory

The need of the supply inventory is defined by the following purposes. First, *to separate operations* of the production and distribution processes. Such separation is necessary because these two processes are not always exactly synchronized. Inventory is also defined *to meet variation in product demands* in the sense that the demand is usually not exactly known, and a safety stock must be maintained in response to its variation. Moreover, it is defined in order *to meet price changes* to take advantage of possible quantity discounts and, finally, *to provide variation in raw material* delivery time caused by unexpected events of the existing defected materials, a stock shortage at the vendors' plants or also in the shipping time variations.

For each of the proceeding inventory purposes, taking a decision that affects the inventory size depends on the following inventory costs:

– the ordering costs that refer to the managerial costs dedicated to preparing the purchase of an order. Ordering costs include all the details, such as counting items and calculating order quantities; The costs associated with the exchange cost of business data between the operated entities are also included in the ordering costs;

– the storage costs include the costs for storage of the inventories in the warehouses, insurance and taxes. In fact, such costs affect the inventory management in the sense that high holding costs tends to favor low inventory levels and frequent replenishment;

– the shortage costs include costs to fill a delay or cancellation of a given request. There is a trade-off between carrying stock to satisfy demand and the costs resulting from stock outs and backorders.

Establishing the correct quantity to order from vendors or the size of lots submitted to the firm's productive facilities involves a search for the minimum total cost resulting from the combined effects of four individual costs: ordering costs, storage costs and shortage costs. Of course, the timing of these orders is a critical factor that may impact inventory cost. We present in the next section the modeling of inventory control.

5.4. Inventory modeling

An inventory modeling provides the operating policies for maintaining and controlling goods to be ordered and stocked. Such modeling is responsible for ordering and receipt of goods: timing the order placement and keeping track of what has been ordered, how much and from whom. There are several objectives of inventory management:

– minimization of the inventory investment;

– determination of the right level of customer service;

– balance of supply and demand;

– minimization of procurement costs and carrying costs;

– maintenance of an up-to-date inventory control system.

5.4.1. *Terminology*

The inventory problem can be stated in terms of input and output data:

Input data:	***Output data:***
q the ordered quantity	TC the total cost
d the annual demand	EOQ the optimal order quantity
a the fixed ordering cost for each order	T the order cycle time
h the unit holding cost	N the number of orders
p the purchasing cost	

where the total cost is expressed in terms of the ordering, holding and production costs as follows:

$$TC = PC + OC + HC \qquad [5.1]$$

$$TC = \underbrace{pd}_{PC} + \underbrace{a\frac{d}{q}}_{OC} + \underbrace{h\frac{q}{2}}_{HC} \qquad [5.2]$$

5.4.2. *Economic order quantity model*

The problem for inventory management is, when ordering supplies, to determine what quantity of a given product to order. Many formulas and algorithms have dealt with this problem. Of these the simplest formula is the most used: the economic order quantity (EOQ) or Lot Size formula. [HAD 63] covers many assumptions of the EOQ.

Let us assume that we are interested in optimal inventory policies for widgets. The EOQ formula uses four variables. They are:

– q order quantity. This is the variable we want to optimize. All the other variables are fixed quantities;

– a fixed ordering cost. This includes the fees charged for making any order and is independent of q;

– h warehousing charge per year per unit of inventory.

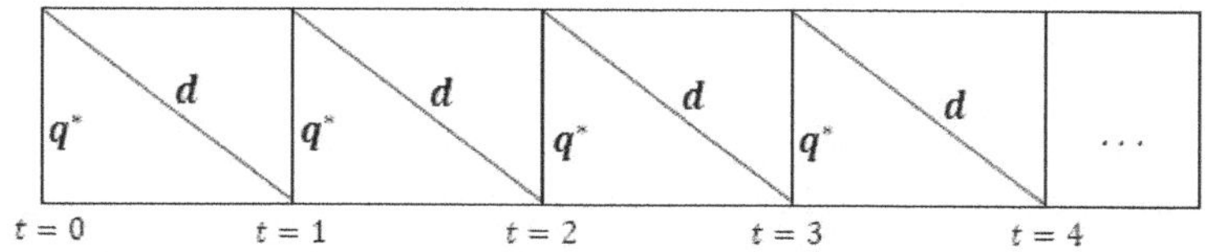

Figure 5.2. *The EOQ process*

The EOQ problem can be summarized as determining the order quantity q^*, that balances the order cost a and the holding costs h in order to minimize total costs. The greater q^* is, the less the company will order and the more it spends for storage. As showed by Figure 5.2, the basic EOQ model assumes that orders for inventories arrive instantly and all at once. Then, the customers' demand is perfectly steady.

In order to compute the EOQ that corresponds to the optimal quantity to be ordered, the more convenient way is to consider Q as the only variable in [5.2] and derive the optimal quantity to be addressed. To do so, we proceed to differentiate [5.2] and set it to 0, as reported in equation [5.3]:

$$0 = -\frac{da}{q^2} + \frac{h}{2} \qquad [5.3]$$

Therefore, the economic order quantity is:

$$q^* = \sqrt{\frac{2da}{h}} \qquad [5.4]$$

The optimal number of orders per year is:

$$T = \frac{d}{q^*} \qquad [5.5]$$

The interval between orders is assumed to be as follows:

$$T = \frac{q^*}{d} \qquad [5.6]$$

5.4.3. *Examples*

1) Suppose:

d = annual demand = 2000 $

q = ordered quantity = 200 $

a = fixed ordering cost = 20 $

h = warehousing charge per year per unit of inventory = 64

p = sale price per unit= 30 $

Following equation [5.2], the total inventory cost is:

$$TC = 30 \times 2000 + 20 \times \frac{2000}{200} + 64 \times \frac{200}{2} = 66.600$$

The economic order quantity is as follows:

$$q^* = \sqrt{\frac{2 \times 2000 \times 20}{64}} = 35.35$$

The optimal interval of reordering is:

$$T = \frac{35.35}{2000} = 0.017\ years, 0.017 \times 365 \approx 7\ days$$

Hence, the company will order every week.

2) A firm has 1,000 A items (which it counts every week, i.e., 5 days), 4,000 B items (counted every 40 days), and 8,000 C items (counted every 100 days). How many items should be counted per day?

Item Class	Quantity	Policy	Number of Items to Count Per Day
A	1,000	Every 5 days	$\frac{1000}{5} = 200$
B	4,000	Every 40 days	$\frac{4000}{40} = 100$
C	8,000	Every 100 days	$\frac{8000}{100} = 80$
			Total items to count: 380

3) Assume you have a product with the following parameters:

Annual demand = 360 units

Holding cost per year = 1.00 per unit

Order cost = 100 per order

What is the EOQ for this product?

$$EOQ = \sqrt{\frac{2 \times demand \times order\ \ cost}{holding\ \ cost}}$$

$$= \sqrt{\frac{2 \times 360 \times 100}{1}} = \sqrt{72000} = 286.33$$

The EOQ model assumes that any real quantity is feasible. The actual quantity ordered may need to be an integer value and may be affected by packaging or other item characteristics. In the following problems, an EOQ of 268 is assumed.

4) Given the data from problem 3, and assuming a 300-day work year, how many orders should be processed per year? What is the expected time between orders?

$$N = \frac{Demand}{Ordered\ quantity} = \frac{360}{268} = 1.34\ orders\ per\ year$$

$$N = \frac{Ordered\ quantity}{Demand} = \frac{268}{360} = 0.74 \quad \times 365 = 271.72$$
$$days\ between\ orders$$

5) What is the total cost for the inventory policy used in problem 3?

$$TC = Order\ cost \times \frac{Demand}{Ordered\ quantity} + Holding\ cost$$
$$\times \frac{Ordered\ quantity}{2} = 360 \times \frac{100}{268} + 1 \times \frac{268}{2} = 268$$

6) Based on the material from problems 3–5, what would be the cost if the demand was actually higher than estimated (i.e., 500 units instead of 360 units), but the EOQ established in problem 3 above is used? What will be the actual annual total cost?

$$TC = Order\ cost \times \frac{Demand}{Ordered\ quantity}$$
$$+ Holding\ cost \times \frac{Ordered\ quantity}{2}$$
$$= 500 \times \frac{100}{268} + 1 \times \frac{268}{2} = 320.57$$

5.5. Conclusion

The inventory problem, considered as a key activity in the SC, requires the definition of a series of data inputs from the three main entities of the SC, namely suppliers, retailers and customers. The inventory management consists of answering how often to review the stock status, when to order new quantity and how much quantity to be ordered in order to save the total inventory cost. In fact, the inventory management is defined as a system that supervises the flow of inventories from the suppliers to the customers through a set of intermediate warehouses. We presented in this chapter the economic order quantity as a simplest model that responds to the purposes of inventory management. Mainly, to determine the optimal quantity to be ordered, the number of orders and the time between orders.

6

The Delivery in the Supply Chain

6.1. Introduction

Today's complex global supply chains are full of uncertainty. The volatile economic environment and customer demand variability require supply chains to be able to anticipate, control and react to disruptions and volatility, in collaboration with customers, suppliers and logistics partners. In order to restore supply chain stability, companies are looking for ways to optimize their global supply chain operations to execute on a customer value strategy of selling and fulfilling the right products and services at the right price, place and time. Transportation is one of these world players that have a daily struggle to offer their customers not only the best products but also the best experience, at the right time, price and quality. The main purpose in the delivery activity is to optimize the transfers between all sites that can produce different varieties of items and make sure they are available in the right quantities demanded at the right point of sale. Traditionally, two alternative objective are considered: the minimization of the total distance traveled or the minimization of the total travel cost. This minimization is subject to system constraint as the route continuity, the delivery to each customer once and the fulfillment of trucks' capacity limitations. The delivery problem thereby specified gives rise to a routing solution that uses a subset of the available trucks while detailing each truck's pathway. We explain in this chapter the different transportation versions that may be addressed and the main benefits of an optimization process in the resolution of such a mathematical modeling. As pointed out in Figure 6.1, two delivery protocols are addressed:

– $Delivery_1$ *[Suppliers - Firms]* Once orders are launched to the suppliers, a delivery strategy should be studied for the storage of orders in firms' warehouses. Hence, given warehouses' locations and available suppliers' trucks, a cost saving delivery plan is output while respecting structural routing constraints. Figure 6.1 reports a plotting of the delivery protocol between suppliers and firms' warehouses, termed as "Delivery 1", that enables the storage of ordered items.

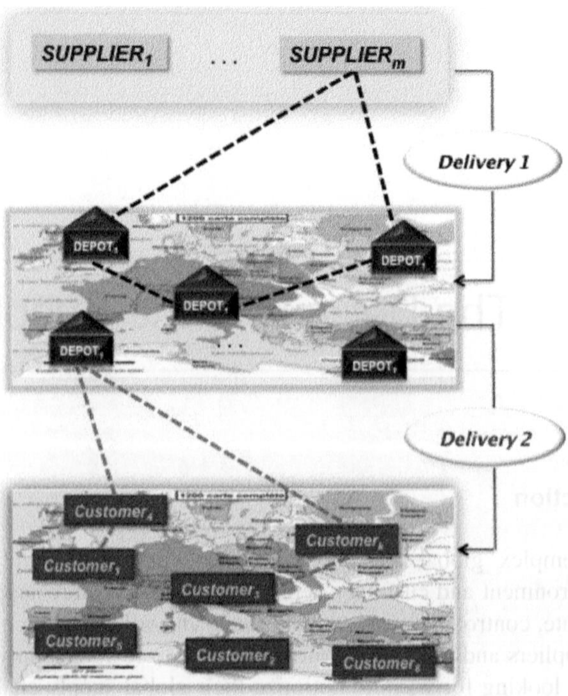

Figure 6.1. *The delivery process in the SC*

– *Delivery*$_2$ *[Firms - Customers]* Customer orders already stored in the warehouses are to be delivered to the final customers while minimizing the total delivery cost. Figure 6.1 clearly illustrates the two SC levels involved in the "Delivery 2" and shows the impact of an optimization of the delivery plan which has a great impact on the traveled distance and the trucks used for the delivery, knowing that the number of customers is relatively large.

We analyze in the subsequent of this chapter the "Delivery 2" routing class due to its impact in the performance of the SC and its influence in the minimization of the total cost incurred by all SC partners.

The present chapter is split into following sections. Section 6.2 outlines the main steps of the delivery process in the SC starting from the acceptance of orders from suppliers to the statement of the best routing solution. Section 6.3 states the delivery problem, its terminology, inputs/outputs and its two main routing variants. Section 6.4 discusses the first variant named the delivery with capacitated trucks. Section 6.5 defines the second variant termed the delivery with times windows. For each problem variant, we state its mathematical programming formulation followed by its problem parameters and decision variables. This chapter is enclosed by an illustrative delivery case study.

6.2. The delivery process in the SC

The delivery in the SC consists of specifying:

– a warehouse that constitutes a procurement source for customers' orders;

– the set of customers to be served, their locations and their demands;

– a set of trucks to be used for the delivery of orders.

Hence, given such input data, the basic delivery process consists of minimizing the travel distance of the set of trucks used, while fulfilling routing constraints.

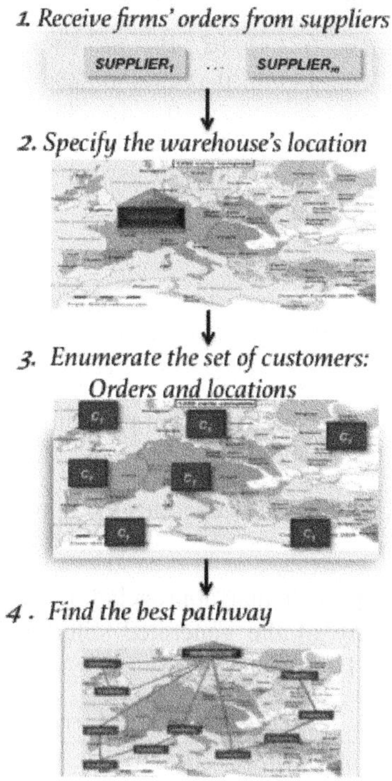

Figure 6.2. *The delivery process in the SC*

Figure 6.2 displays the main steps of the delivery process. We detail below the main steps to be followed, as reported in Figure 6.2, for a cost saving delivery process:

1) *Receive firms' orders from suppliers:* ordered items are received in firms' warehouses for final deliveries to customers. The assignment of appropriate warehouses for the reception of orders is planned in such a way as to be close the set of customers to be served.

2) *Specify the warehouse's location:* extract the geographical coordinates of the addressed warehouse. The position of the warehouse is part of the distance matrix to be input for solving the delivery problem.

3) *List the set of customers: orders and locations*: once the set of customers to be served is specified, their geographical coordinates are then extracted from the original distance already created using customers' geographical coordinates. This is done using Google Maps API that computes the Euclidean distance between all pairs of vertices (the set of customers and the depot). Hence, a distance matrix is extracted as the following:

	Depot	1	2	3	4	...
Depot	0	14	45	38	70	
1	14	0	29	60	46	
2	45	29	0	16	89	
3	38	60	16	0	57	
4	70	46	89	57	0	
⋮						⋱

The demand of each customer is also provided to make sure that trucks' capacity limits are respected.

4) *Find the best pathway*: depending on the problem size, the delivery problem is solved using:

– an optimizer, as CPLEX, that generates the optimal solution for small sized instances;

– an approximate approach that approaches the optimal solution versus an infinitesimal gap. The quality of the generated solution measured by this gap is formulated as in equation [6.1].

$$Gap = \frac{Approximate\ \ solution - Optimal\ \ solution}{Approximate\ \ solution} \times 100 \qquad [6.1]$$

6.3. Problem description

Figure 6.1 displays the basic scheme that points out a central depot containing all customer orders and a routing plan, that delivers all customer orders, consisting of three pathways (drawn in green, red and blue).

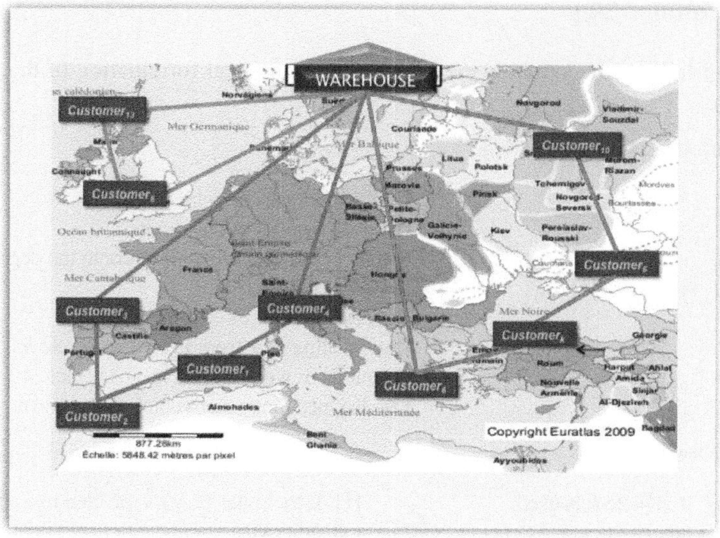

Figure 6.3. *The delivery process in the SC. For a color version of the figure, see www.iste.co.uk/krichen/supplychain.zip*

The CVRP is expressed as a connected graph $G = (V, E)$ such that:

– V: is the set of selling points and the depot;

– E: express the distances of direct routes between each pair of connected vertices.

The delivery of orders, designed as a connected graph, is shown in Figure 6.4, where $|V| = 6$ and $|E| = \frac{\sum_{i=1}^{6} deg(i)}{2} = \frac{4+3+3+3+4+3}{2} = 10$ edges.

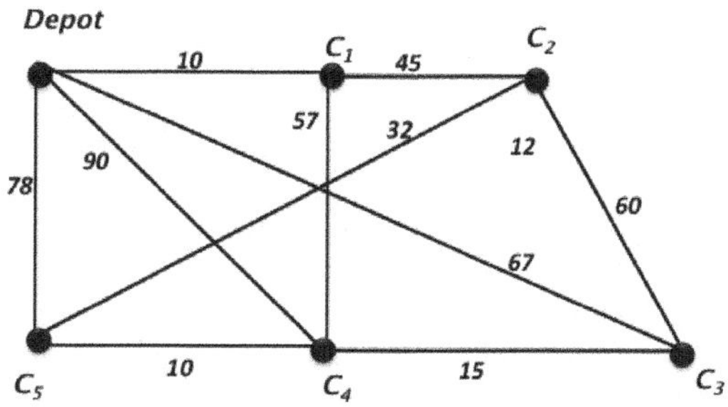

Figure 6.4. *Graph modeling of the delivery problem*

6.3.1. *Terminology*

There follows the symbols used for the mathematical formulation of the delivery problem:

– Parameters

n	The total number of vehicles
m	The total number of customers
$V = \{0, \ldots, m\}$	The set of vertices where 0 refers to the depot
$E = \{\{i, j\} : i, j \in V\}$	The set of edges
w_j	The order weight of customer j
c_{ij}^k	The traveling cost from i to j by vehicle k
$[w_{min}^k, w_{max}^k]$	The range of weight capacity for vehicle k
$[d_{min}^k, d_{max}^k]$	The distance range that vehicle k can travel

– Decision variables

$$y_k = \begin{cases} 1 \text{ if vehicle } k \text{ is used} \\ 0 \text{ otherwise} \end{cases} \qquad x_{ij}^k = \begin{cases} 1 \text{ if the route } \{i, j\} \text{is traveled by vehicle } k \\ 0 \text{ otherwise} \end{cases}$$

6.3.2. *Inputs/outputs of the delivery*

The inputs and outputs of the DP are reported hereafter:

Inputs	*Outputs*
n: the number of customers' orders	$y_j = \begin{cases} 1 \text{ if truck } j \text{ is used} \\ 0 \text{ otherwise} \end{cases}$
v: the number of vehicles W_j the capacity of vehicle j w_i: the weight of customer i's order	
	$x_{ij}^k = \begin{cases} 1 \text{ if the route } \{i, j\} \text{ is traveled by vehicle } k \\ 0 \text{ otherwise} \end{cases}$

6.3.3. *Delivery variants*

Numerous routing variants are relevant in the delivery of customers' orders, namely the capacitated vehicle routing problem (CVRP) [TLI 13] that tries to reach the most cost saving solution while satisfying routing constraints and respecting trucks' capacities. The second routing variant called the vehicle routing problem with time windows (VRPTW) ([KRI 14b]) takes into account, besides the routing constraints, time window restrictions required from customers for the delivery of launched orders.

6.4. First variant: delivery with capacitated trucks

This delivery problem also called the CVRP consists of finding least cost routes for a heterogeneous fleet of vehicles that schedule their departures from a single depot to a set of geographically dispersed selling points. Each customer has his specific order to be delivered by one of the vehicles.

	CAPACITATED VEHICLE ROUTING PROBLEM	VEHICLE ROUTING PROBLEM WITH TIME WINDOWS
	CVRP	*VRPTW*
OBJECTIVE	*Minimize the total travel cost*	*Minimize the total travel cost*
SYSTEM CONSTRAINTS	*– Routing constraints* *– Trucks capacities' limits*	*– Routing constraints* *– Time windows requirements*

6.4.1. *CVRP specification*

The textual formulation of the CVRP is written as follows:

Min the total traveling cost
S.t.
- *Each customer is served by exactly one vehicle*
- *Each route starts and ends at the depot*
- *The weight and distance capacity of each vehicle should be respected*

First, SC inputs are to be provided: customers' demands and locations are to be specified as well as the distance matrix in order to determine the vehicles' travel costs. Once the transport network is created, the warehouse, also called the depot, should contain all customers' orders to be distributed using numerous vehicles' pathways.

6.4.2. *Mathematical formulation of the CVRP*

Based on the above mentioned assumptions in the specification (section 6.5.1), the mathematical formulation of the CVRP with the vehicles' weight capacities is written as follows [TLI 14]:

– the objective function of delivery model [6.2] tries to minimize the total routing cost;

– the first set of constraints of [6.2] expresses that each travel should start and end at the depot;

– the second set of constraints in optimization model [6.2] guarantees that each customer is served by exactly one vehicle;

– the third set of requirements corresponds to the typical flow conservation equation that ensures the continuity of each vehicle's route;

– the subtour elimination is presented by the fourth set of constraints;

– the maximum capacity of a vehicle as well as its traveled distance belongs to an allowed range, as reported respectively in the last set of constraints of model [6.2];

$$
\begin{aligned}
&Min\ z(x) = \textstyle\sum_{i=1}^{n} \sum_{j=1}^{n} \sum_{k=1}^{v} c_{ij}^{k} x_{ij}^{k} \\
&S.t. \\
&\quad \textstyle\sum_{j=1}^{v} x_{0j}^{k} = 1 \quad k = 1, ..., v \\
&\quad \textstyle\sum_{i=1}^{v} x_{i0}^{k} = 1 \quad k = 0, ..., v \\
&\quad \textstyle\sum_{i=0}^{v} \sum_{k=1}^{n} \sum_{i \neq j, j=0}^{max} x_{ij}^{k} = 1 \ j = 1, \ldots, n \\
&\quad \textstyle\sum_{i=0}^{v} x_{ij}^{k} - \sum_{i=0}^{v} x_{ji}^{k} = 1, \ j = 1, \ldots, n, \ k = 1, \ldots, v \\
&\quad \textstyle\sum_{i \in S} \sum_{j \in S} x_{ij}^{k} \leq |S| - 1, k = 1, \ldots, v, \forall S \subseteq V, |S| \in \{2, \ldots, n\} \\
&\quad w_{min}^{k} y^{k} \leq \textstyle\sum_{i=0}^{v} \sum_{j \neq i, j=0}^{v} w_j x_{ij}^{k} \leq w_{max}^{k} y^{k}, \ k = 1, \ldots, v \\
&\quad x_{ij}^{k}, y^{k} \in \{0, 1\}, i = 0, \ldots, n, \ j = 1, \ldots, n, \ k = 1, \ldots, v
\end{aligned}
\qquad [6.2]
$$

6.5. Second variant: delivery with time windows

The second delivery variant consists of minimizing the total travel routing cost while assuming that time windows for the delivery are imposed by the customers. Based on such assumptions, additional time constraints are to be added to the basic routing model.

6.5.1. *VRPTW specification*

Hence, the textual formulation of the delivery problem with time windows is written as follows:

Min the total traveling cost
S.t.

– *each customer is served by exactly one vehicle*;
– *each route starts and ends at the depot*;
– *each customer's order should be delivered within the required time windows*;
– *the weight and distance capacity of each vehicle should be respected.*

Given here is a complete directed graph $G = (V, E)$ where

– $V = \{0, 1, ..., n\}$ of vertices;

– $E = \{(i, j)|i, j \in V, i \neq j\}$ of edges connecting the customers.

With each customer i is associated a fixed demand d_i $(d_i > 0)$ of goods to be delivered within a time window $[e_i, l_i]$ and a service duration s_i. With each edge $\{i, j\}$ $\in E$ is associated a cost c_{ij} and a travel time t_{ij} ($c_{ij} \geq 0$ and $t_{ij} \geq 0$). The set of available trucks denoted by $T = \{1,2,...,v\}$ is also specified and followed by the trucks' capacities W, assumed to be identical. In this version of the delivery problem, the number of vehicles is fixed in advance and it is required that each customer i is served by exactly one vehicle within a time window.

6.5.2. *Mathematical formulation of the VRPTW*

The mathematical programming formulation can be written as follows:

$$
\begin{aligned}
& Min\ z(x) = \textstyle\sum_{i=1}^{n} \sum_{j=1}^{n} c_{ij} \sum_{k=1}^{v} x_{ij}^{k} \\
& S.t. \\
& \qquad \textstyle\sum_{i=1}^{n} \sum_{k=1}^{v} x_{ij}^{k} = 1 && 1 \leq j \leq n \\
& \qquad \textstyle\sum_{j=1}^{n} \sum_{k=1}^{v} x_{ij}^{k} = 1 && 1 \leq i \leq n \\
& \qquad \textstyle\sum_{i=1}^{n} \sum_{l=1}^{n} x_{il}^{k} = \sum_{j=1}^{n} \sum_{l=1}^{n} x_{ljk} \\
& \qquad \textstyle\sum_{j=1}^{n} x_{0j}^{k} = 1 && 1 \leq k \leq m \\
& \qquad \textstyle\sum_{i=1}^{n} x_{i0}^{k} = 1 && 1 \leq k \leq m \\
& \qquad \textstyle\sum_{i=1}^{n} \sum_{j=1}^{n} x_{ij}^{k} \leq W_k && 1 \leq k \leq v \\
& \qquad x_{ij}^{k}(s_{ik} + t_{ij} - s_{jk}) \leq 0 \\
& \qquad a_i \leq s_{ik} \leq b_i \\
& \qquad x_{ij}^{k} \in \{0, 1\} && 1 \leq i, j \leq n; 1 \leq k \leq v
\end{aligned}
\qquad [6.3]
$$

– the objective function of delivery model [6.2] represents the total travel cost to be minimized;

– the first and the second set of constraints mean that every customer $i \in \{V \setminus 0\}$ must be served exactly once by a vehicle;

– the third set of constraints preserve the vehicle fleet;

– the fourth and fifth set of constraints ensure that each tour starts and ends at the depot;

– the rest of the constraints ensure that capacity limitations and time requirements are respected.

6.6. A real case study: the case of Tunisia

Let us consider a delivery problem that includes $n = 9$ customers to be satisfied by $k = 4$ identical trucks. Each vehicle has a maximum capacity $W = 1800$.

The inputs/outputs of the delivery problem

Inputs	*Outputs*
$n = 9$	$y_{j\,(j=1,\ldots,4)} = \begin{cases} 1 & \text{if truck } j \text{ is used} \\ 0 & \text{otherwise} \end{cases}$
$v = 4$ $C_{(9\times 9)}$: cost matrix	
$(W_1, W_2, W_3, W_4) = (1800, 1800, 1800, 1800)$	$x^k_{ij\,(i,\ j=1\ldots,6,\ k=1,\ldots 4)} = \begin{cases} 1 & \text{if the route } \{i, j\} \text{ is traveled by vehicle } k \\ 0 & \text{otherwise} \end{cases}$

Order	O_1	O_2	O_3	O_4	O_5	O_6	O_7	O_8	O_9
w_i	220	150	100	500	300	150	250	500	770

The cost matrix C is reported as follows:

$$\begin{pmatrix}
 & D & c_1 & c_2 & c_3 & c_4 & c_5 & c_6 & c_7 & c_8 & c_9 \\
D & 0 & 37.27 & 37.22 & 37.43 & 37.24 & 37.67 & 37.80 & 38.03 & 38.16 & 39.86 \\
c_1 & & 0 & 37.05 & 37.70 & 37.45 & 37.97 & 38.04 & 38.38 & 38.24 & 39.58 \\
c_2 & & & 0 & 37.65 & 37.40 & 37.90 & 38.03 & 38.38 & 38.25 & 39.53 \\
c_3 & & & & 0 & 37.25 & 37.30 & 37.37 & 37.73 & 37.61 & 38.88 \\
c_4 & & & & & 0 & 37.56 & 37.63 & 37.98 & 37.86 & 38.62 \\
c_5 & & & & & & 0 & 37.13 & 37.48 & 37.36 & 38.06 \\
c_6 & & & & & & & 0 & 37.35 & 37.23 & 37.93 \\
c_7 & & & & & & & & 0 & 37.12 & 37.58 \\
c_8 & & & & & & & & & 0 & 37.70 \\
c_9 & & & & & & & & & & 0
\end{pmatrix}$$

The optimal solution generated by the optimizer CPLEX uses two trucks out of four. Subsequently,

– *used trucks:* $(y_1, y_2, y_3, y_4) = (1, 1, 0, 0) \Rightarrow \sum_{j=1}^{4} y_j = 2$

– *truck 1:* $\boxed{D} \xrightarrow{37.22} \boxed{C2} \xrightarrow{37.05} \boxed{C1} \xrightarrow{37.45} \boxed{C4} \xrightarrow{37.56} \boxed{C5}$

– *truck 2:* $\boxed{D} \xrightarrow{37.43} \boxed{C3} \xrightarrow{37.37} \boxed{C6} \xrightarrow{37.23} \boxed{C8} \xrightarrow{37.12} \boxed{C7} \xrightarrow{37.58} \boxed{C9}$

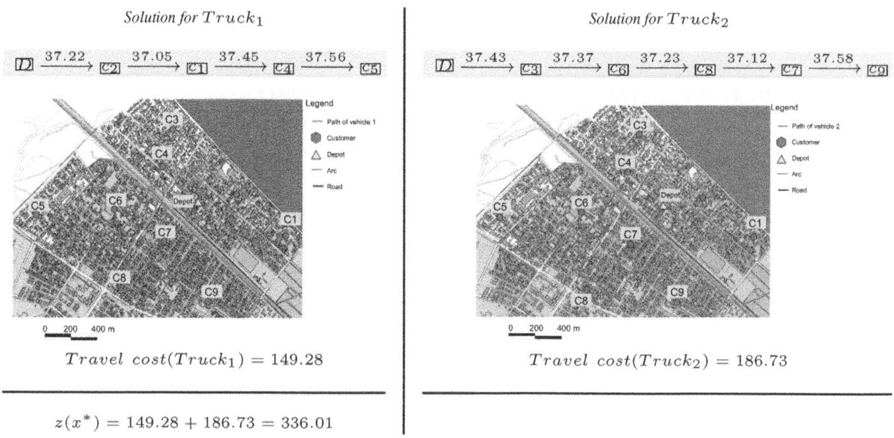

Figure 6.5. *Delivery solution for truck 1 and truck 2*

6.7. Alternative resolution approaches for the delivery problem

6.7.1. *A tabu search approach for solving the delivery problem*

The tabu search (TS) metaheuristic first proposed by [GLO 90] was extensively used to solve hard constrained optimization problems, especially routing problems. Due to its capability in escaping local optima by the use a tabu list and the neighborhood generation, it performs well in generating promising solutions in a reasonable computation time. The main components involved in the TS algorithm are:

– the initial solution generation;

– the neighborhood exploration;

– the tabu list that forbids going back to already visited solutions during a predefined number of iterations;

– the diversification process;

– the intensification process;

– the stopping criteria.

The TS approach proceeds iteratively by an alternative use of alternative neighborhoods in order to diversify the search by exploring different areas of the feasible set. All TS parameters were set after a meta-tuning. Once the numerical solution is generated, the DSS moves to the design of the cartographical solution that clearly illustrates the real itinerary. Customers' locations are then marked in the addressed area and vehicles' pathways are highlighted.

Algorithm 4: A tabu search algorithm for the delivery process

---

Require: $cmd \leftarrow list\ of\ commands$, $C \leftarrow capacity$, $LISTT \leftarrow NULL$, $Matrix \leftarrow list\ of\ distances$

Find the initial solution S_0 using a greedy-based algorithm

$S^* \leftarrow S_0$, $nb \leftarrow 0$, $c^* \leftarrow f(s_0)$

while $Time \leq T_{max}$ **do**

  $s = exchange(s^*)$ and s not in $LISTT$

  if($f(s) < c^*$) then

  $s^* \leftarrow s$

  $f^* \leftarrow f(s)$

  Update LISTT

  $s = insertion(s^*)$ and s not in $LISTT$

  if($f(s) < c^*$) then

  $s^* \leftarrow s$

  $f^* \leftarrow f(s)$

  Update LISTT

end while

6.7.2. *A genetic algorithm for solving the delivery problem*

Genetic algorithms (GAs) are likely to be the most widely known metaheuristic algorithms for efficiently solving NP-hard optimization problems, today receiving remarkable attention all over the world. GAs are computer procedures that employ the mechanics of natural selection and natural genetics to make solutions evolve efficiently. The basic concepts of GA were applied to numerous combinatorial optimization problems. Such a metaheuristic is a population-based iterative approach that handles a set of chromosomes in order to output, after a prefixed number of iterations, an improved solution while applying genetic operators. Experimental results on real instances have shown the capability of such approaches in generating powerful solutions. Each chromosome has a fitness value associated with it, and a set of best fit chromosomes from each generation survive into the next generation.

6.7.2.1. *Solution encoding*

A solution to the delivery problem can be modeled as an array where each position i informs about the involved customers that are handled by each vehicle. The depot is symbolized as "0". The encoding of a solution is the following:

0	2	6	...	4	0	1

The above solution indicates that $truck_1$ delivers for customers $2, 6, \ldots, 4$, and so on.

6.7.2.2. *Crossover*

One way for improving the solution quality of currently evaluated solutions is the use of the crossover operation that consists of combining the gene chains of two selected chromosomes to output new chromosomes. The crossover can be simple or multiple. Simple crossover consists of exchanging portions of the two chains in a single point while the second point includes several points of crossing. For the sake of simplicity, we use the one-point crossover that selects two chromosomes, then exchange the two portions in order to obtain new solutions. The process can be described as follows:

(a) | (b)

0	2	5	6	9	0	1

(c) | (d)

0	1	2	0	10	8	0

$(a) + (d)$

0	2	5	0	10	8	0

$(c) + (b)$

0	1	2	6	9	0	1

6.7.2.3. *Mutation*

The mutation operator inverses two genes randomly, corresponding to the assignment of two randomly selected items. Their re-assignment can yield to an improvement of the solution.

0	↓ 7	9	0	1	↓ 5	0

In the above scheme, customers 7 and 5 are selected for the mutation. The exchange of the two genes makes customer 5 served by $truck_1$ and customer 7 served by $truck_2$.

Algorithm 5: The genetic algorithm for the delivery process

1: Generate a population of individuals of size N: x_1, x_2,. . ., x_N (an initial solution).
2: Calculate the probability of survival (quality or fitness) of each individual:$f(x_1)$, $f(x_2)$,. . ., $f(x_N)$.
3: Check if the criterion of termination is reached. If so, go to finish.
4: Choose a pair of individuals for the reproduction (according to the chances of survival of each individual).
5: According to the probabilities associated with each genetic operator, apply these operators.
6: Place the individuals produced in the new population.
7: Check if the size of the new population is correct. If not, return to step 4.
8: Replace the former population of individuals by the new one.
9: Return to step 2.

6.8. A DSS design for the delivery problem

Due to its importance in the SC performance and cost influence, it is highly recommended to use an electronic platform, known as a decision support system (DSS), that facilitates the delivery of orders. We discuss hereafter a DSS [FAI 14] and [FAI 12] for the delivery in the SC.

INTERFACE 1

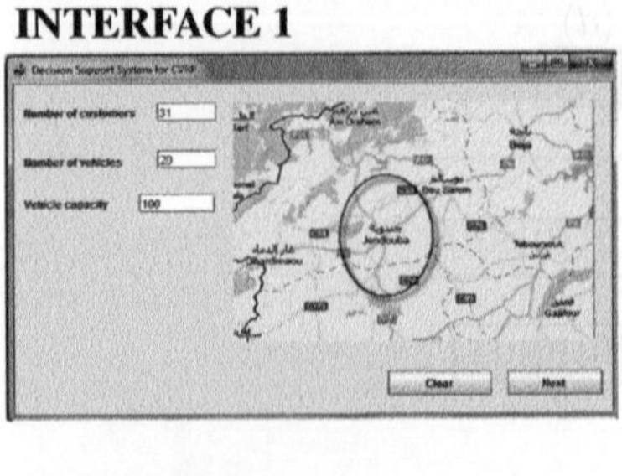

INTERFACE 2

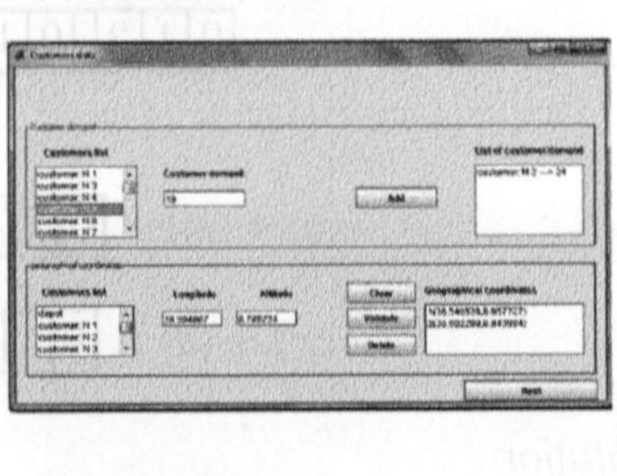

INTERFACE 3

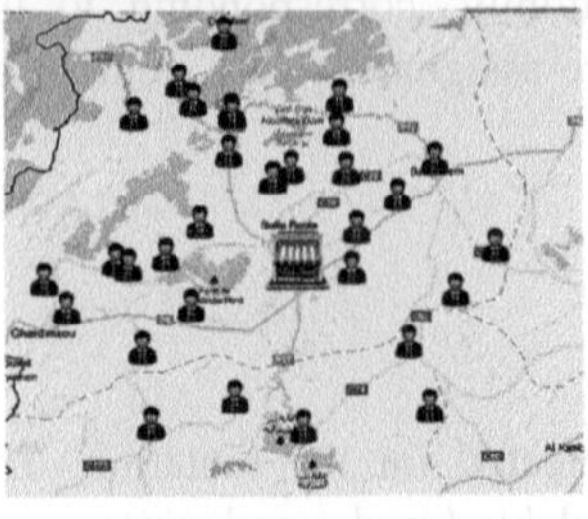

INTERFACE 4

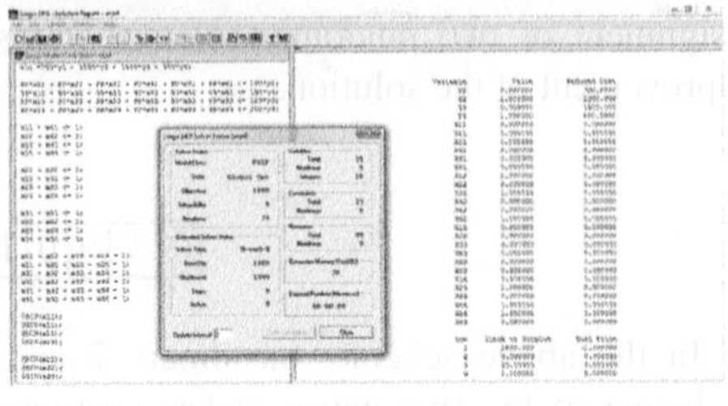

INTERFACE 5

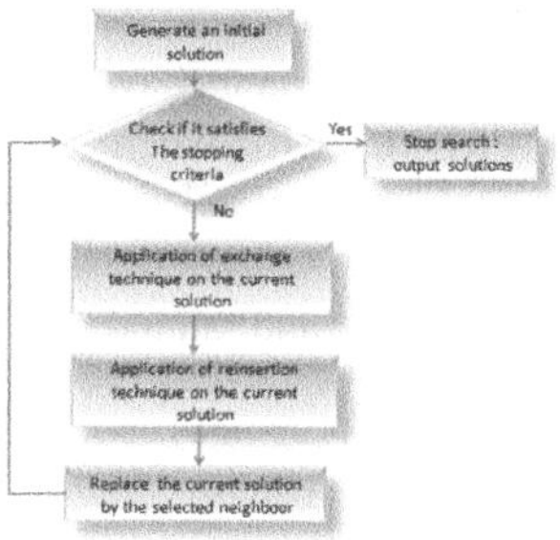

INTERFACE 6

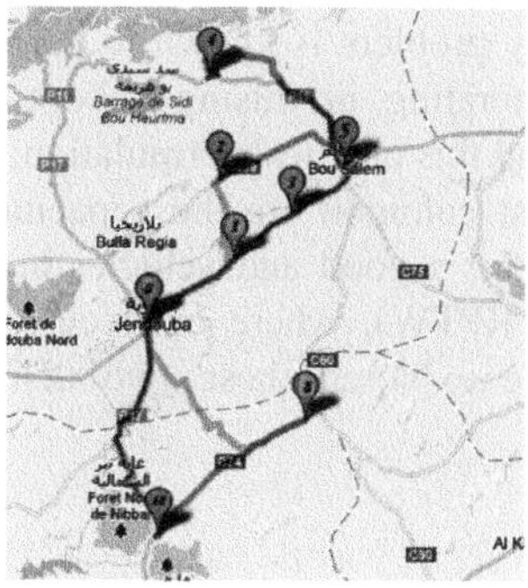

Figure 6.6. *Process flow of the delivery problem*

COMMENTS ON FIGURE 6.6.

1) *INTERFACE 1*: the first interface inputs the basic data such as the number of customers and available trucks followed by their characteristics.

2) *INTERFACE 2*: the second screen inputs customers' positioning coordinates, demands and time frames for their delivery.

3) *INTERFACE 3*: the third interface locates, using Google maps, the geographical position of the involved customers on the map.

4) *INTERFACE 4*: given all data inputs, the fourth interface performs the CPLEX optimizer to generate the optimal solution of the delivery instance using the previously input data.

5) *INTERFACE 5*: the DSS can solve the delivery instance heuristically by performing an approximate approach such as the tabu search metaheuristic.

6) *INTERFACE 6*: the solution is then output in a geographical format showing the pathway of each truck used.

6.9. Conclusion

The delivery problem in the SC is a combinatorial optimization and integer programming problem seeking to service a number of customers with a fleet of vehicles. This challenging problem, first proposed by Dantzig and Ramser back in 1959, consists of a stream of strategic decisions within the SC. The delivery problem consists of transporting items to some geographically dispersed customers using a set of vehicles operating from a single depot. The objective of the delivery problem is to serve a set of customers with known demands on minimum cost vehicle routes originating and terminating at the depot. The problem is then expressed in terms of decision variables, parameters for those variables and constraints between those variables. As the delivery problem is known to be $\mathcal{NP}$-hard, approximate methods perform well when generating promising suboptimal solutions in a reasonable computation time. Beyond this classical formulation, a number of variants have been studied. Among the most common are the capacitated VRP (CVRP), where each customer has a demand for a good and vehicles have finite capacity and the VRP with Time Windows (VRPTW), where each customer must be visited during a specific time frame. We explored these two delivery variants and stated their mathematical models.

Bibliography

[ANS 12] ANSTREICHER K., "Interior-point algorithms for a generalization of linear programming and weighted centering", *Optimization Methods and Software*, vol. 27, nos. 4–5, pp. 605-612, 2012.

[AUM 74] AUMANN R., DREZE J., "Cooperative games with coalition structures", *International Journal of Game Theory*, Physica-Verlag, vol. 3, no. 4, pp. 217–237, 1974.

[BEA 08] BEAL S., DURIEU J., SOLAL P., "Farsighted coalitional stability in TU-games", *Mathematical Social Sciences*, vol. 56, no. 3, pp. 303–313, 2008.

[BEL 06] BELMONTE M.-V., CONEJO R., DE-LA CRUZ J.-L.P. *et al.*, "Coalitions among intelligent agents: a tractable case", *Computational Intelligence*, vol. 22, no. 1, pp. 52–68, 2006.

[BEN 15] BEN JOUIDA S., OUNI A., KRICHEN S., "A Multi-start Tabu Search Based Algorithm for Solving the Warehousing Problem with Conflict", *Modeling, Computation and Optimization in Information Systems and Management Sciences*, Springer International Publishing, vol. 360, pp. 117–128, 2015.

[BER 11] BERMAN O., DREZNER Z., KRASS D., "Discrete cooperative covering problems", *Journal of the Operational Research Society*, vol. 62, no. 11, pp. 2002–2012, 2011.

[BLO 96] BLOCH F., "Sequential formation of coalitions in games with externalities and fixed payoff division", *Games and Economic Behavior*, vol. 14, no. 1, pp. 90–123, 1996.

[BRA 07] BRANDENBURGER A., "The power of paradox: some recent developments in interactive epistemology", *International Journal of Game Theory*, vol. 35, no. 4, pp. 465–492, 2007.

[BÜR 12] BÜRGER M., NOTARSTEFANO G., BULLO F. *et al.*, "A distributed simplex algorithm for degenerate linear programs and multi-agent assignments", *Automatica*, vol. 48, no. 9, pp. 2298–2304, 2012.

[CAC 99] CACHON G.P., ZIPKIN P.H., "Competitive and cooperative inventory policies in a two-stage supply chain", *Management Science*, vol. 45, no. 7, pp. 936–953, July 1999.

[CAR 10] CARDINAL J., HOEFER M., "Non-cooperative facility location and covering games", *Theoretical Computer Science*, vol. 411, no. 16–18, pp. 1855–1876, 2010.

[COO 11] COOK W., KOCH T., STEFFY D. *et al.*, "An exact rational mixed-integer programming solver", *Integer Programming and Combinatorial Optimization*, Notes in Computer Science, Springer Berlin Heidelberg, vol. 6655, pp. 104–116, 2011.

[DAN 04] DANG V.D., JENNINGS N.R., "Generating coalition structures with finite bound from the optimal guarantees", *Proceedings of the 3rd International Joint Conference on Autonomous Agents and Multiagent Systems - Volume 2*, AAMAS '04, Washington, DC, IEEE Computer Society, pp. 564–571, 2004.

[FAI 12] FAIZ S., KRICHEN S., *Geographical Information Systems and Spatial Optimization*, Taylor & Francis, 2012.

[FAI 14] FAIZ S., KRICHEN S., INOUBLI W., "A {DSS} based on {GIS} and Tabu search for solving the CVRP: the Tunisian case", *The Egyptian Journal of Remote Sensing and Space Science*, vol. 17, no. 1, pp. 105–110, 2014.

[GAR 79] GAREY M.R., JOHNSON D.S., *Computers and Intractability: A Guide to the Theory of NP-Completeness*, W. H. Freeman, 1979.

[GAR 11] GARCIA-VILLORIA A., SALHI S., COROMINAS A. *et al.*, "Hyper-heuristic approaches for the response time variability problem", *European Journal of Operational Research*, vol. 211, no. 1, pp. 160–169, 2011.

[GEO 95] GEOFFRION A.M., POWERS R.F., "Twenty years of strategic distribution system design: An evolutionary perspective", *Interfaces* 25, vol. 5, pp. 105–127, 1995.

[GIL 59] GILLIES D.B., "Solutions to general non-zero-sum games", *Contributions to the Theory of Games IV*, Annals of Mathematics Studies, Princeton University Press, Princeton, no. 40, pp. 47–85, 1959.

[GLO 90] GLOVER F., "Tabu search: a tutorial", *Interfaces*, vol. 20, pp. 74–94, 1990.

[HAD 63] HADLEY G., WHITIN T., *Analysis of Inventory Systems*, Prentice-Hall International Series in Management, Prentice-Hall, 1963.

[HEN 97] HENIG M., GERCHAK Y., ERNST R. *et al.*, "An inventory model embedded in designing a supply contract", *Management Science*, vol. 43, no. 2, pp. 184–189, 1997.

[KAH 84] KAHAN J.P., RAPOPORT A., *Theories of Coalition Formation*, L. Erlbaum Associates, 1984.

[KLI 10] KLIBI W., MARTEL A., GUITOUNI A., "The design of robust value-creating supply chain networks: a critical review", *European Journal of Operational Research*, vol. 203, no. 2, pp. 283–293, 2010.

[KRI 14a] KRICHEN S., CHAOUACHI J., *Graph-Related Optimization and Decision Support Systems*, ISTE, London and John Wiley and Sons, New York, 2014.

[KRI 14b] KRICHEN S., FAIZ S., TLILI T. *et al.*, "Tabu-based GIS for solving the vehicle routing problem", *Expert Syst. Appl.*, vol. 41, no. 14, pp. 6483–6493, 2014.

[LAR 00] LARSON K.S., SANDHOLM T.W., "Anytime coalition structure generation: an average case study", *Journal of Experimental and Theoretical AI*, vol. 12, pp. 40–47, 2000.

[LEE 92] LEE H.L., BILLINGTON C., "Managing supply chain inventory: pitfalls and opportunities", *Sloan Management Review*, vol. 33, no. 3, pp. 65–73, 1992.

[LEE 93] LEE H.L., BILLINGTON C., "Material management in decentralized supply chains", *Operations Research*, vol. 41, no. 5, pp. 835–847, September 1993.

[MAR 03] MARINI M., CURRARINI S., A sequential approach to the characteristic function and the core in games with externalities, MPRA paper, University Library of Munich, Germany, 2003.

[PAP 82] PAPADIMITRIOU C.H., STEIGLITZ K., *Combinatorial Optimization: Algorithms and Complexity*, Prentice-Hall, Inc., Upper Saddle River, NJ, 1982.

[SAN 99] SANDHOLM T., LARSON K., ANDERSSON M. *et al.*, "Coalition structure generation with worst case guarantees", *Artificial Intelligence*, vol. 111, no. 1–2, pp. 209–238, 1999.

[SCH 12] SCHRODL H., "*Adoption of cloud computing in supply chain management solutions: A SCOR-aligned assessment*", *Web Technologies and Applications*, Lecture Notes in Computer Science, Springer Berlin Heidelberg, vol. 7234, pp. 233–244, 2012.

[SEN 00] SEN S., SEN I., DUTTA P.S., "Searching for optimal coalition structures", *Proceedings of the 4th International Conference on Multiagent Systems*, IEEE, pp. 286–292, 2000.

[SHA 53] SHAPLEY L., "A value for n-person games", *Contributions to the Theory of Games*, Princeton University Press, vol. 2, pp. 307–317, 1953.

[SHA 71] SHAPLEY L., "Cores of convex games", *International Journal of Game Theory*, Physica-Verlag, vol. 1, no. 1, pp. 11–26, 1971.

[STE 68] STEARNS R., "Convergent transfer schemes for n-person games", *Transactions of the American Mathematical Society*, vol. 134, pp. 449–459, 1968.

[TLI 13] TLILI T., KRICHEN S., FAIZ S., "Towards a decision making support system for the capacitated vehicle routing problem", *International Journal of Decision Support System Technology*, vol. 5, no. 4, pp. 21–33, 2013.

[TLI 14] TLILI T., KRICHEN S., FAÏZ S., "Simulated annealing-based decision support system for routing problems", *2014 IEEE International Conference on Systems, Man, and Cybernetics, SMC 2014,* San Diego, CA,pp. 2954–2958, 5–8 October 2014.

[TSA 99] TSAY A.A., "The quantity flexibility contract and supplier-customer incentives", *Management Science*, vol. 45, no. 10, 1999.

[WAN 04] WANG G., HUANG S.H., DISMUKES J.P., "Product-driven supply chain selection using integrated multi-criteria decision-making methodology", *International Journal of Production Economics*, vol. 91, no. 1, pp. 1–15, 2004.

[WAN 14] WANG X., TURETKEN E., FLEURET F. *et al.*, *Tracking Interacting Objects Optimally Using Integer Programming*, of *Lecture Notes in Computer Science*, Springer International Publishing, vol. 8689, 2014.

[YAN 07] YANG J., LUO Z., "Coalition formation mechanism in multi-agent systems based on genetic algorithms", *Applied Soft Computing*, Elsevier Science Publishers B. V., vol. 7, no. 2, pp. 561–568, March 2007.

Index

Index

Other titles from

ISTE

in

Information Systems, Web and Pervasive Computing

2015

ARDUIN Pierre-Emmanuel, GRUNDSTEIN Michel, ROSENTHAL-SABROUX Camille
Information and Knowledge System

BÉRANGER Jérôme
Medical Information Systems Ethics

IAFRATE Fernando
From Big Data to Smart Data

POMEROL Jean-Charles, EPELBOIN Yves, THOURY Claire
MOOCs

SALLES Maryse
Decision-Making and the Information System

2014

DINET Jérôme
Information Retrieval in Digital Environments

HÉNO Raphaële, CHANDELIER Laure
3D Modeling of Buildings: Outstanding Sites

KEMBELLEC Gérald, CHARTRON Ghislaine, SALEH Imad
Recommender Systems

MATHIAN Hélène, SANDERS Lena
Spatio-temporal Approaches: Geographic Objects and Change Process

PLANTIN Jean-Christophe
Participatory Mapping

VENTRE Daniel
Chinese Cybersecurity and Defense

2013

BERNIK Igor
Cybercrime and Cyberwarfare

CAPET Philippe, DELAVALLADE Thomas
Information Evaluation

LEBRATY Jean-Fabrice, LOBRE-LEBRATY Katia
Crowdsourcing: One Step Beyond

SALLABERRY Christian
Geographical Information Retrieval in Textual Corpora

2012

BUCHER Bénédicte, LE BER Florence
Innovative Software Development in GIS

GAUSSIER Eric, YVON François
Textual Information Access

STOCKINGER Peter
Audiovisual Archives: Digital Text and Discourse Analysis

VENTRE Daniel
Cyber Conflict

2011

BANOS Arnaud, THÉVENIN Thomas
Geographical Information and Urban Transport Systems

DAUPHINÉ André
Fractal Geography

LEMBERGER Pirmin, MOREL Mederic
Managing Complexity of Information Systems

STOCKINGER Peter
Introduction to Audiovisual Archives

STOCKINGER Peter
Digital Audiovisual Archives

VENTRE Daniel
Cyberwar and Information Warfare

2010

BONNET Pierre
Enterprise Data Governance

BRUNET Roger
Sustainable Geography

CARREGA Pierre
Geographical Information and Climatology

CAUVIN Colette, ESCOBAR Francisco, SERRADJ Aziz
Thematic Cartography – 3-volume series
Thematic Cartography and Transformations – volume 1
Cartography and the Impact of the Quantitative Revolution – volume 2
New Approaches in Thematic Cartography – volume 3

LANGLOIS Patrice
Simulation of Complex Systems in GIS

MATHIS Philippe
Graphs and Networks – 2nd edition

THÉRIAULT Marius, DES ROSIERS François
Modeling Urban Dynamics

2009

BONNET Pierre, DETAVERNIER Jean-Michel, VAUQUIER Dominique
Sustainable IT Architecture: the Progressive Way of Overhauling Information Systems with SOA

PAPY Fabrice
Information Science

RIVARD François, ABOU HARB Georges, MERET Philippe
The Transverse Information System

ROCHE Stéphane, CARON Claude
Organizational Facets of GIS

VENTRE Daniel
Information Warfare

2008

BRUGNOT Gérard
Spatial Management of Risks

FINKE Gerd
Operations Research and Networks

GUERMOND Yves
Modeling Process in Geography

KANEVSKI Michael
Advanced Mapping of Environmental Data

MANOUVRIER Bernard, LAURENT Ménard
Application Integration: EAI, B2B, BPM and SOA

PAPY Fabrice
Digital Libraries

2007

DOBESCH Hartwig, DUMOLARD Pierre, DYRAS Izabela
Spatial Interpolation for Climate Data

SANDERS Lena
Models in Spatial Analysis

2006

CLIQUET Gérard
Geomarketing

CORNIOU Jean-Pierre
Looking Back and Going Forward in IT

DEVILLERS Rodolphe, JEANSOULIN Robert
Fundamentals of Spatial Data Quality

Printed and bound by CPI Group (UK) Ltd, Croydon, CR0 4YY

13/09/2026

14961018-0001